Henry II and the Angevin Empire 1154-1189:

A Study Guide for AS/A Level

Table of contents

Introductory Notes

Henry II and the Angevin Empire (1154-1189): A Study guide for AS/A Level

This study guide will assist you in your AS/A Level studies of Medieval History; the reign of King Henry II and the Angevin Empire, a period of study that focuses on the years 1154-1189.

Henry II is a monarch that deserves study. He greatly transformed and expanded the power of kings in England and made the English throne prominent throughout Europe. His methods and policies helped England to rapidly recover from the period of Anarchy that plagued the reign of his immediate predecessor on the English throne.

The aims and objectives of Advanced Level GCE in History include;

- Develop an interest in and enthusiasm for history and an understanding of its intrinsic value and significance.
- Acquire an understanding of different identities within society and an appreciation of aspects such as social, cultural, religious and ethnic diversity, as appropriate.
- Build on your understanding of the past through experiencing a broad and balanced course of study.
- Improve as an effective and independent learner.
- Develop the ability to ask relevant and significant questions about the past and to research these questions.
- Acquire an understanding of the nature of historical study.
- Develop your use and understanding of historical terms, concepts and skills.
- Make links and draw comparisons within and/or across different periods and aspects of the past.
- Organise and communicate your historical knowledge and understanding in different ways, arguing a case and reaching substantiated judgements.

Studying GCE History

This study guide has been written to provide a rewarding experience for those who are, or are interested in studying Medieval History. In particular, this study guide will assist you in understanding and examining the subject matter of the reign of Henry II and the Angevin Empire.

Who is this study guide for?

This study guide is intended to offer a satisfying experience for those learners who undertake an AS or A level qualification in History. This qualification pathway is offered by Edexcel, AQA or OCR examination boards and this resource is primarily designed to assist those who are studying this topic for a History qualification.

This study guide will help to lay a sound foundation for those who go on to study the Medieval World at a higher (degree) level as well as appeal to those who are interested in learning more about the medieval world generally and in particular, the establishment of the Kingdom of England and the Angevin Empire

Please note that this study guide is not endorsed either by AQA or OCR and as such is not an officially recognised product by Edexcel, AQA, OCR or CIE examination boards.

This product is designed to be used as a study aid in order for learners to attain a qualification in the following examination units;

Edexcel Examination Board

- **Level 3 Advanced GCE in History (9HIO): Route A**
- **Level 3 Advanced Subsidiary (AS) GCE in History (8HIO): Route A**

AQA Examination Board

- **Advanced Level GCE in History (7042): Component 2A**
- **Advanced Subsidiary (AS) Level GCE in History (7041): Component 2A**

How to use this guide

This A Level study guide has been organised in such a way so as to help an A Level student of medieval history more easily understand the life and career of Henry II and also to correspond to the major topic areas identified by the major examination boards.

To this end this Athena Critical Guide is divided into four ***Parts*** each containing five ***sections*** that relate to the overall theme of the relevant Part. Each subsection discusses a specific aspect or series of related aspects relevant to the A level student, so for example Part Two relates to the early years of Henry II's reign and each section deals with a specific aspect as identified below;

Part Two: King Henry II: the early years 1154-72

2.1 Henry II, King of England 1154

2.2 Asserting the power of the King 1154-1160: England

2.3 Asserting the power of the King 1154-1160: Europe

2.4 Thomas Becket

2.5 Henry II: Authority and challenges in the years 1161-1172

Each section is introduced with a number of bullet points that will help the reader to identify the focus of the section and also to help correlate the section to their relevant examination specification.

Within each subsection are a number of tasks and activities as well as glossary terms and additional points of information that are considered useful to an A Level student.

The tasks and activities are based on the structure and duration of questions posed by the examination boards therefore it is envisaged that they will be especially valuable in aiding the reader to prepare for their respective examinations.

PART ONE: The makings of a king 1133-1154

PART ONE:

1.1 Europe in 1150: A brief introduction

1.2 The state of affairs in England and Normandy 1100-1148

1.3 The early years of Henry 1133-1154

1.4 Henry and Eleanor of Aquitaine -1152

1.5 Henry and Stephen 1153-1154

1.1 Europe in 1150: A brief introduction

In this section we will;

- *Explore and understand the geography and major political institutions of Western Europe around 1150*
- *Explore the characteristics of Nobles and Knights in Europe*
- *Investigate the traits of Nobility*

The Geography of Europe in 1150

Cities in 1150AD

Approximate populations;

Baghdad – *500,000*

Cairo – *450,000*

Cologne – *20,000*

Constantinople 600,000

Cordoba – *100,000*

Florence – *40,000*

London – *20,000*

Milan – *30,000*

Paris – *20,000*

Rome – *35,000*

Venice – *40,000*

The region was dominated by two faiths, Christianity and Islam.

The Old Roman Empire had been transformed, and not destroyed in 410AD with the sack of Rome. No longer centred in Rome, the Roman Empire had survived and even flourished in the East; a substantial part of the region depicted in this map was ruled by the Greek speaking successor to Rome; known commonly as, if somewhat misleadingly, as the Byzantine Empire. The Byzantine Empire was situated between the Danube River in the North and the Taurus Mountains in the East; with its capital in a central position called Constantinople; modern Istanbul.

Further North and West lay the 'Holy Roman Empire'. Rather than a unified Empire of Romans united in holiness, the Holy Roman Empire was a series of semi-independent dukedoms and counties located in central Europe; much of which is in Germany today. The ruler of the Holy Roman Empire claimed to be the direct inheritor of the Roman Empire in the West; a claim substantiated by, or challenged by, the Pope on many occasions. Further West was France, whose king likewise struggled to maintain control of many great lords.

In Northern Italy city states were emerging as powerful polities in their own right, some ruled by dynastic families, others as republics. These city states were dependent or independent of their larger neighbours as the scales of balance of politics shifted. In Sicily and Southern Italy Norman adventurers were in the process of carving out their own kingdom at the expense of both the Byzantine Empire whose hold on Southern Italy was being eroded as well as Muslim rulers of cities in Sicily.

The British Isles were dominated by the Anglo-Norman kingdom of England which had been conquered by the Normans in 1066 after the battle of Hastings. In Ireland, Scotland and Wales the land was ruled by many clan chiefs and tribal kings, but increasingly the Normans were penetrating into these lands too and acquiring lands and authority.

In the Iberian peninsular the relatively new Christian statelets of Castile, Leon, Aragon, Navarre and Portugal were expanding their territory at the expense of each other as well as the independent Muslim *Taifa* kingdoms that remained after the Umayyad Caliphate crumbled in the early part of the 11th century.

To the East the Abbasid Caliphate commanded the actual or nominal allegiance of much of Syria, Iraq and Iran from their capital at Baghdad, but their rule was faltering as local Emirs refused to send their regular tribute to their distant overlord. The Sunni Arab Caliph was increasingly dependent upon Turkish Sultan who held the real power. To the South the rival Shi'ite Caliphate of the Fatamids was based in Egypt and commanded much of Palestine and Southern Syria.

In Central and Eastern parts of Europe lived peoples newly converted to Christianity, such as Slavic peoples in the Balkans, Poland and parts of southern Russia and Ukraine. In Hungary the Magyars had settled in the old Roman province of Pannonia after centuries of migration and established a new and energetic kingdom both courted and contested by their neighbours in the Byzantine and Holy Roman Empires.

Groups of people continued to migrate throughout this period. Normans and Scandinavians sought land in several regions and the men of these peoples often served as mercenaries in the Byzantine Empire or for a minor lord. In a general migration from Central Asia, Turkish tribes, such as the Pechenegs headed west, some passing north of the Black Sea and putting pressure on the Danube frontier of the Byzantine Empire, or the eastern regions of the Holy Roman Empire. Other Turkish groups moved into lands ruled by the Abbasid caliphate, here they were converted to Sunni Islam and would become key players in the crusades.

In 1150 AD most Christian countries the majority of the inhabitants were Christian, there were a few Jewish communities settled in towns along the trade routes which connected the West to the East. In contrast, the territories controlled by Muslim rulers had much greater diversity of religion amongst their populations. Christian communities of many sects existed alongside Jewish communities under Muslim rule and whilst some persecution occurred at times, these communities often thrived.

In general, at the time of the 1st Crusade, which occurred between the years 1095-1100, the cities of the East were much larger in size and splendour than the cities in the West. Some old cities like Rome had gone into decline in the West, however the city of Cordoba in what is now southern Spain had by far the largest population amongst the cities in the West.

In the 1050s the Seljuk Turks had become the effective rulers of the Abbasid Caliphate. Taking the title of *Sultan* ('Power' in Arabic), the Seljuks would rule in all but name in Iraq and Syria and decisively defeat the Byzantine Empire at the battle of Manzikert in 1071 that would enable Turkish groups to migrate into Anatolia. One of the indirect consequences of this battle would be the 1st Crusade.

Nobles and Knights in Europe

The development of kingdoms in Europe such as the kingdoms of England and France depended to a great extent on the complex relationships between Rulers and Nobles, the relationships between Nobles and Nobles and the relationships between Nobles and non-nobles.

A King or Noble (or someone who aspired to be either) needed certain requirements in order to maintain or improve their standing including;

- *The trait of nobility*
- *A family name*
- *Primogeniture and Inheritance*
- *Land acquisition*
- *Military skill and reputation*
- *A fortified home; a Castle*
- *Knights*

It is important to understand that these pressures motivated many lords (and those who aspired to become lords and nobles) during the 12th century and kings were under tremendous pressure to provide land and wealth for their supporters. If the claims of a lord were ignored or overlooked in these regards, then this was often a major cause of dissatisfaction and could and did lead to rebellion. As we shall see, even the sons of Kings were subject to these pressures.

The trait of nobility?

Straightaway here we run into a potential problem; *nobility* is a term that in practice is not easily defined or applied. Some people might be described as noble due to their birth into a family of nobles; others might equally be defined as noble through their virtues and moral behaviour. In the loosest terms of definition we could perhaps equate the trait of nobility with links to families of power and status within a given area.

Nobles could be described as those who managed to acquire control or ownership of a castle or town or could even be used to describe anyone who was born as a 'Freeman'. This could therefore even include very poor peasants that lived in areas not under the control of any 'Overlord'. The definition then is loose, subject to change and prone to misconceptions.

One common misconception of nobility then was that with nobility came wealth. This misconception is false. Baldwin I (king of Jerusalem) for example was relatively poor before he joined the First Crusade. Another misconception that commonly occurs is that a knight by definition must be noble. This was never the case. The status of fighting men was often equated with being a knight; yet there were many kinds of fighting men who came from many different backgrounds. Soldiers of the Byzantine Empire for example might come from peasant families who were obligated to provide their own horse and weapons, but were not described as knights.

A family name

A Noble ideally possessed a family name; they could link themselves through their family tree and ancestry to men and families of wealth and status. In an ideal world a noble would be able to point to their family tree and identify a link of either blood or marriage ties to the idealised Christian king that united much of Europe in the late 8th and early 9th centuries under his rule; Charlemagne.

Another way to acquire the trait of nobility was to marry into a family that already possessed this trait. Many nobles had daughters that required marrying off and, whilst many of these daughters married other noble families, occasions did occur when a noble lord would permit his daughter to marry someone from a much less illustrious background. Sometimes these were the youngest sons of lords who had little to recommend them except their family name, but sometimes a lord may allow his daughter to marry non-nobles of wealth and means, such as merchants or even peasants that had acquired wealth and success. This strategy of marrying noble to money had its dangers however, having ancestors of poor or servile origins in your family tree could jeopardise your own nobility. In the early 11th century for example, the Count of Flanders, desperate for additional funds threatened to strip the land and assets of noble families within his county that had any suggestion of non-noble origins.

Primogeniture and Inheritance

Anyone born into a noble family could easily describe themselves as 'noble', however, all too often these 'nobles' lacked the other necessities required to truly merit the accolade of being a noble. Much of what was missing was wealth and land.

When a noble lord died, it was often the case that all of the deceased wealth and lands and titles went solely to the eldest male child. Other children, male and female, would not inherit anything. This rule of inheritance is known as *Primogeniture*.

Whilst female children were typically married off to remove them from the household (and to create links with other families), younger male children were either left with the choice of joining the Church as priest (hoping in turn to gain the wealth and status that came from high churchly rank), staying at the side of their brother as a sometimes reluctant and unwanted house guest, or leaving home to seek land and wealth elsewhere.

More often, a noble would inherit something from their father's lands and wealth; it might be a manor house or a small castle on the edges of the family land. In any event, in order to be granted this land or possession, the second or third son would be required to perform an act of homage to their sibling, who became their liege lord. Sometimes this grant of land and home would be too small to satisfy the ambitions and hope of the younger or ousted child.

The case of William Marshall (1147-1219)

William Marshall was born around 1147, the second son of John Marshall, a middling noble who possessed lands in Berkshire and Wiltshire. William was sent to Normandy as a teenager in order to learn the ways of knighthood. Acquiring a skill in arms in battle and through successes in tournaments across France, William Marshall acquired fame but not land. After being wounded by the men of Guy of Lusignan in a skirmish in Poitiers, Marshall was appointed to serve as a household knight retainer of Henry the Young King. After the death of the Young King in 1183, Marshall travelled to the Holy land before entering the service of Henry II himself and served him loyally until Henry II's death in 1189.

Despite charging Richard in battle and killing his horse in defence of King Henry II in 1189, Richard bore William Marshall no grudge and promoted him soon after by marrying him to a wealthy heiress on the Welsh border and through this marriage William Marshall acquired the earldom of Pembroke in Wales and also land in Normandy and Ireland. Almost overnight, William Marshall went from landless knight to one of the great landowners of the Angevin Empire.

William Marshall was appointed co-justiciar of England during Richard's absence during the Third Crusade and after Richard's death served King John loyally despite many reasons to rebel until King John's death in 1216. Thereafter William Marshall served as regent to John's son and heir, winning a war and implementing Magna Carta until William Marshall himself died in 1219 of natural causes.

Land acquisition

In Medieval Europe, much of what we understand as wealth could actually be translated as 'land'. Land was the basis of almost all economies in Western Europe. Land was used to grow crops and rear livestock on, which all who lived in the area depended upon for sustenance and the slight hope of improving their wealth. Without land, a noble had no real means to generate income and therefore maintain their standing in society. Land could be used by nobles to generate wealth as well as to meet the obligations imposed upon them by their overlords. Land could be used to reward followers with and could be increased.

Policies and tactics which nobles could use to increase their ownership of land included;

- De-forestation, land drainage and reclamation works - (much land in Europe in the late 11th century was uncultivated and needed only to be cleared and settled in order to be acquired). This method would be time consuming and expensive.

- Serve a lord in return for them granting you land – this technique would usually result in the land being granted conditionally and may not be permanent. As a poorer noble, you might already own land elsewhere which would also have conditions attached to it. What if your overlords disagree? You might have to serve one against the other.

- Emigration - Nobles needed to be able to provide for themselves and their followers, and this provision often came from the acquisition of land. If a noble could not inherit land, they could emigrate to other parts of the world and gain land through service elsewhere where they were encouraged to journey to. Many French nobles moved to England for example after 1066, whilst others took up service in the kingdom of Sicily or in the Byzantine Empire.

- Seizing land from non-Christians - one option for a landless noble was to try and take land from others by force. The Eastern areas of Europe where pagan peoples still lived was one area exploited by German nobles in particular. French (particularly from the southern parts of France) were encouraged to participate in the wars in Spain between Christian and Muslim rulers in the hope of gaining land.

- Seizing land from your neighbours - a final option for the landless noble of Western Europe was to raid neighbouring lordships in the hope of acquiring some wealth through plunder or event to forcibly seize parts of their territory.

Many of these methods of land acquisition required the aspiring noble to be able to fight.

Military skill and reputation

Kings and great lords were required to be military leaders in practice. Their claims to large areas of lands and wealth would be jeopardised by a reluctance to, or inability to fight. If a noble had a great reputation as a warrior it could deter others from seeking to exploit them. However, a poor military reputation and numerous defeats could be an invitation for others to try and take advantage.

In order for a king or lord to fight then, it follows that they required the means to be able to fight. A retinue of armed warriors was an essential must have for a lord or noble. This armed retinue likewise had to be skilled in battle and or of sufficient size so that when conflict occurred, the lord could lead his men to victory. This armed retinue could either be paid in cash, paid in booty and plunder acquired by force, or paid for in land. The armed forces of a lord might be recruited as mercenaries from other areas, be men obligated to serve from the lord's territories or may be landless nobles hoping to acquire land through service to another.

Knights and Castles

In Medieval Europe, war was typically fought in order to achieve one of the following aims;

- Plunder
- Conquest

In order for the war mongering noble to succeed in the attack the noble needed a core of professional force of armed fighting men – what we might call knights. For a noble to be able to protect his possessions, a noble would need not only a force of professional force of armed fighting men, but also means of defence to protect his valuables. A common means of defence was to safeguard wealth in fortified locations – castles.

When we think of knights we must not think of King Arthur and his Knights of the Round Table. Brave in battle, courteous to women and the poor and galloping around on white horses in shiny silvered armour. Whilst this was the image that many knights would like to portray it is far from accurate.

Knights were trained mounted soldiers, but they were almost certainly less than courteous to the poor and the vulnerable. Indeed, their favourite targets in war were often precisely the poor and defenceless. These were rough men, used to fighting in all conditions against other rough men. They were armoured (usually with types of chainmail armour) and equipped with lances, spears, swords and a variety of blunt objects such as hammers and maces which they used to knock each other from their horses (which too had been trained to fight in battle and were also sometimes armoured). Knights were recruited from a variety of backgrounds, from the local nobility for certain, but also illegitimate sons of nobles, as well as men from the fields that their neighbours and lords knew had an aptitude for violent work. Landless nobles from other areas too would flock to regions beset by violence in the hope of gaining employment, bringing with them little but the possessions that their animals and few retainers could carry and there training in the ways of medieval warfare. Despite being in the minority on any given battlefield, the knights could fight off many times their numbers of badly equipped and nonskilled foot soldiers.

Castles were fortified places, areas from which the noble could stay relatively safe whilst under attack, house his property and keep supplies of food. They also provided a focal point for the noble's lands and a place where the affairs of his land (law courts and business) might also take place.

Castles could be built of earth, timber or stone and could be small or large in size. Some castles were very simple, a wooden fence atop a hill of earth, others were extremely elaborate, capable of housing hundreds of people in times of danger and having their own community in their own right. A Noble might require a stone castle – from either the grounds of prestige or necessity, but a stone castle could take years to construct and was extremely expensive. A noble might pay for a castle by increasing the taxation on his subjects, borrowing money or acquiring the wealth through attacks on their neighbours.

An individual with luck, skill or determination then could be created through the acquisition of land, a castle and a retinue of knights. He might construct a crude castle close to a road, people it with a group of local toughs and prey on the inhabitants and trade passing through a local area. The locals might pay off the bully in the castle in return for peace, whilst at the same time the king or overlord may overlook the behaviour of the bully in the castle in return of some service, money or acknowledgment of over lordship, with such acknowledgment comes nobility, and within a relatively short amount of time, an area might have a new noble lord.

The aspirations of the landless noble and the needs and requirements of the lords of the land therefore intertwined. Lords had land, men and castles, without these a lord, no matter how noble, was not a lord. Landless nobles neither land, men nor castles, but were usually better placed than those without nobility to acquire these from those that did.

Task: Ranking exercise: Traits of nobility?

Look again at the characteristics discussed earlier;

- *A family name*
- *Primogeniture and Inheritance*
- *Land acquisition*
- *Military skill and reputation*
- *A fortified home; a Castle*
- *A retinue of Knights*

Which of these characteristics do you think is the most important requirement for someone to be considered as a Noble in Europe during the 12th century?

Spend no more than 30 minutes on this task

1.2 The state of affairs in England and Normandy 1100-1148

In this section we will;

- *Explore the major historical events of the years 1100-1148*
- *Consider why the reigns of King Henry I and King Stephen were so problematic*
- *Investigate the period of civil war known as 'The Anarchy'*
- *Understand the circumstances of the birth and connections of the future King Henry II*

King Henry I of England 1100-1135

Henry I was the fourth son of William the Conqueror and was born in 1068, after William had been crowned King of the English. When William the Conqueror died in 1087, Henry was given a large sum of silver, some £5,000, but no lands. Henry could have decided to address this issue of land by joining the First Crusade like his brother Robert of Normandy. Instead Henry elected to remain in England within the household of his other brother; William II of England.

William II died in 1100 during a bizarre hunting accident that may or may not have been deliberately arranged. Henry was present at the event and moved swiftly in order to secure the throne of England, despite his elder brother Robert, Duke of Normandy travelling home from Palestine after the successful conclusion of the First Crusade.

Henry was crowned King of the English in 1100 and succeeded in not only keeping Robert out of England, but was able to invade and conquering Normandy and capture Duke Robert in 1106, who would spend the rest of his life in comfortable imprisonment in Cardiff.

In 1100 Henry I issued a coronation charter which abolished the 'evil customs' of his brother William II. Henry I's charter dealt with issues such as the rights of widows and under age heirs to land and inheritances, debts, wills, royal forest rights, and fines (*amercements*) and taxes (*relief*) payable by barons and earls.

All did not go smoothly for Henry I however, in 1120 his only legitimate son and heir, William died during a drunken sailing accident, thereafter Henry I would spend much of his energy attempting to secure a new heir. Despite being the father of some twenty two acknowledged illegitimate children, he remained without a legitimate son, his only legitimate daughter was Matilda and she was married to Emperor Henry V of Germany. Henry V of Germany died in 1125 and Matilda was recalled to her father's household and Henry compelled his barons and earls to accept Matilda as heir to the throne.

Matilda remarried in 1128 to Geoffrey Plantagenet; the heir to the County of Anjou, the implications of this marriage would be lasting and far reaching.

Key term: Angevin and the Angevin dynasty

Throughout this guide we will use the term 'Angevin'. But what does this mean?

In short the term Angevin means *'from Anjou'*.

Amongst modern historians the phrase 'Angevin' is used to refer to the lands and kingdoms of the Angevin kings who are;

- Henry II (1154-1189)
- Richard I (1189-1199)
- John (1199-1216)

Anjou

Anjou is a region in France, positioned approximately in central north western part of the Country France, Anjou lay along the North bank of the river Loire and included towns such as Angers and Le Mans.

The lords of Anjou and Normandy were rivals and this rivalry had often spilled over into war. As a consequence of this rivalry, the rulers of Anjou had a terrible reputation amongst their Norman neighbours. Count Fulk III the Black for example was widely regarded as a rapist and murderer, whose brutality even during the 11th century was remarkable. Henry I himself had fought several wars with the Count of Anjou, yet more recently the family had been viewed as one of the rising stars of Western Europe. Fulk V of Anjou had married his daughter to Henry I's son William in 1119 and after William's death in 1120, Fulk and Henry I had continued to work together against the King of France. A new marriage was arranged in 1128 between Henry I's daughter Matilda and Fulk's son Geoffrey and shortly after this marriage Fulk himself surrendered his County of Anjou to his son so that he could journey to Palestine to become the king of Jerusalem.

In theory all should have been well. Henry I had demanded of his barons that they recognise the rights of his daughter (and her husband) to succeed him after he died. Henry therefore had an heir who could rule his lands however, a good portion of Henry I's Anglo-Norman barons and earls resented the impending rule of the Angevin family. Henry I himself had seized the throne of England, as had his father William the Conqueror. If they could do, this then why not others?

King Stephen 1135-1154

In 1135 King Henry I died. He was succeeded not by Matilda and Geoffrey of Anjou, but rather by Stephen. Stephen's reign would see England and Normandy embroiled in decades of political and social upheaval and a lengthy civil war known as 'The Anarchy'.

King Stephen was a leading Anglo-Norman baron and noble. A younger son of Stephen, Count of Blois and his wife Adele, the daughter of William the Conqueror, Stephen could claim almost as strong a link as his rival Matilda to the crown of England. His father was the same Stephen of Blois who had joined the First Crusade, deserted at Antioch in 1098 and subsequently been forced to return to complete his vow of pilgrimage. This he had done and Count Stephen had restored his reputation through his death in battle in Palestine in 1102.

Stephen himself had not inherited the county of Blois after his father's death, however Stephen had been raised in the household of King Henry I and been rewarded for his service with extensive tracts of lands in both France and England. Another brother; Henry of Blois too had sought favour and patronage in England, he was Bishop of Winchester and also one of the wealthiest men of England in his own right.

In 1135 King Henry I died and Stephen was quick to act. Crossing to England, Stephen had himself crowned on the 22nd December 1135 and received the allegiance of many of the Anglo-Norman barons and earls. Matilda was far removed from England and could not move quickly enough herself to deny Stephen the kingship. For two years, Stephen ruled England a king undisputed. Stephen rewarded his followers well, but in doing so decided to ignore and overlook other important and powerful lords in England, including Robert, the Earl of Gloucester, and an illegitimate son of King Henry I. The years of peace were ended.

By 1138 King Stephen had alienated several important barons and earls and Geoffrey and Matilda had also made preparations to contest King Stephen's rule. Whilst Robert of Gloucester rebelled, Geoffrey of Anjou invaded the Duchy of Normandy and King David of Scotland attacked Northern England.

Civil war erupted and the period known as 'The Anarchy' had begun.

Matilda vs Stephen

> ***Queen Matilda and Empress Matilda***
>
> *As we continue with the discussion of events of the Anarchy, we shall refer to Stephen's wife Matilda as Queen Matilda, whilst Matilda daughter of Henry I we shall refer to by her former title Empress Matilda.*

King Henry I had made his leading lords swear allegiance to Matilda on several occasions, the latest being in 1133 after her marriage to Geoffrey of Anjou had resulted in the birth of the child that would become in time King Henry II. After Henry I's death however, these oaths of allegiance were soon cast aside by many.

In England Matilda was effectively disinherited. Along with her husband in 1135 they only effectively ruled the County of Anjou. In contrast, Stephen had seized England, had secured the loyalty of the lords of Normandy and also held the title of Count of Boulogne as a result of his marriage to wife, Matilda. According to one contemporary source the *Gesta Stephani* (On the Acts of Stephen);

"There was no-one else at hand who could take the king's place and put an end to the great dangers threatening the kingdom."

Empress Matilda was pregnant in 1135 with her third child and could not move rapidly. Whilst Stephen had been on good terms with King Henry I, Matilda and her husband had been involved in a territorial dispute with her father over the issue of a string of castles along the Normandy – Anjou border. This dispute was still unresolved at the time of Henry I's death.

Four ways in which King Stephen contributed to Civil War

With the benefit of hindsight Stephen could have ruled as King relatively securely. As it was Stephen made several key blunders that enabled and encouraged Matilda to contest his ruler-ship as well as his own supporters to turn against him.

First of all Stephen managed to alienate his own brother Henry, the bishop of Winchester. When the most senior Church position in England became vacant, Stephen did not help his brother to secure the post of the Archbishop of Canterbury.

Secondly, King Stephen neglected his lords and lands in Normandy. Stephen is known to have visited Normandy only once, in 1137. Thereafter he made no effort to protect his own interests in Normandy and allowed Count Geoffrey of Anjou to invade Normandy in 1138. By 1144, Normandy was completely lost to King Stephen.

Thirdly, King Stephen dismissed three experienced officials and administrators from their positions in the Royal Chancellery and Treasury. These men were also prominent Church men and by replacing these men with military men with little or no experience of the governance of the kingdom Stephen not only lost this expertise, he also angered the Church, which saw these positions as part of the offices provided to the king by the Church in England.

Finally, King Stephen relied on a small group of supporters to rule in England. He alienated the majority of the powerful barons and earls of England, denying them offices and positions and ignoring their appeals and claims. As a result in 1138 Earl Robert of Gloucester, the most powerful earl in England rebelled and pledged his allegiance to his half-sister, the Empress Matilda.

Task: King Stephen vs Empress Matilda

Who had the best claim to the rulership of England in 1135?

For each of the activities below write 1-2 paragraphs;

- Outline the strengths and weaknesses of the relative positions of Stephen and Matilda.
- Who do you think had the stronger claim to the throne of England? Explain your choice.
- If you were an English baron, who do you think you might have most reason to support?
  Explain your choice.
- If you were a Norman baron, who do you think you might have most reason to support?
  Explain your choice.

The Anarchy 1138-1148

Strictly speaking the war against Stephen's rule began soon after he became King with Geoffrey of Anjou's invasion of Normandy. But the civil war in England only really began in 1138 when Robert, Earl of Gloucester revolted from Stephen's rule. As the most powerful Earl in England (as well as an illegitimate son of King Henry I) it should have been important for King Stephen to foster his support.

After seeking the support of the Pope against King Stephen, the Empress Matilda landed in England in 1139 and established her own court and government at Bristol.

In 1140 the Empress Matilda's supporters, including Earl Robert of Gloucester began large scale raids across England. In the North, King David of Scotland (Matilda's Uncle) joined in the action by invading Northern England. He had soon overrun Northumbria and Cumbria. Stephen in retaliation ordered invasions of his own, however it soon became clear that neither Empress Matilda nor King Stephen could access the resources required to achieve a total victory. The result was a long drawn out conflict in which the suffering inflicted upon the peasants and poor would be severe and extended.

King Stephen however continued to offend those who might otherwise support him. When he refused to give due compensation to Earl Ranulf of Chester, Ranulf rebelled and seized Lincoln Castle. Lincoln Castle was one of the most important places in England during the 12th century and King Stephen led an army personally to recapture the place. In February 1141, as he was laying siege to Lincoln, King Stephen was captured in battle by Earl Robert of Gloucester who attacked him there. This was the moment when Empress Matilda could put an end to the Anarchy. But she failed.

Snatching defeat from victory

The Empress Matilda had a problem; she came across as arrogant and rude. Attempting to address her lack of appeal to the English, she adopted the title of 'Lady of the English' and arranged her triumphal coronation in London. In this she was initially supported by Henry, Bishop of Winchester, but the Empress soon alienated the bishop of Winchester and more importantly, King Stephen's wife, the queen Matilda refused to surrender. Queen Matilda organised the defence of the city and incited the populace to reject Empress Matilda. By the 24th June 1141 Empress Matilda had been forced out of London and besieged in Oxford.

Further mishaps occurred for the Empress. Although she escaped from Oxford in the winter of 1141-1142, Earl Robert of Gloucester was defeated in battle and found himself a prisoner. Without her principal general (Matilda's husband Geoffrey had no inclination to travel to England, he was still concerned with conquering Normandy). The Empress found she could not conduct a military campaign without Earl Robert. An exchange was made; Stephen for Robert.

King Stephen, now released began to go on the offensive; Matilda was forced into the South West corner of England; despite the arrival from Normandy of some assistance of questionable value; 300 knights and her son Henry Fitz Empress, now aged nine.

The state of the lands in the Anarchy

The civil war again reached a stalemate. King Stephen could not force Empress Matilda from the south west. Matilda was discredited by the debacle at London in 1141.

Throughout the Anarchy, local lords and those who aspired to become lords saw opportunity. They could act as the wished with little or no interference from the crown. Lords could exploit the peasantry, build illegal castles to control lands not their own and to tax and constrict any people in the locality. Lords could fight each other and seize land in their own quarrels. Taxes raised for either side were retained by the local lord and spent as he saw fit. As a result England became much poorer and much more dangerous.

Henry FitzEmpress

As we continue with the discussion of events of the Anarchy, we shall refer to the son of Geoffrey of Anjou and Matilda as 'Henry FitzEmpress'.

'FitzEmpress' means 'the son of the Empress'

We cannot call him Henry II yet, because Henry would not be crowned as King of England until 1154.

In the north of England, King David of Scotland had invaded and occupied counties including the regions of Northumbria and Cumbria. He was threatening to come further south.

In Normandy however, the war reached a conclusion in 1144 when Geoffrey of Anjou captured Rouen and effectively had conquered the duchy. This too caused some problems for the nobles in both lands. Many Anglo-Norman lords owned lands in both England and Normandy. As a result they had to swear allegiance to Stephen in England and Geoffrey in Normandy or risk dispossession or some or all of their lands.

Both England and Normandy were shattered and impoverished by the conflict. King Stephen employed additional soldiers from the continent; Flemish mercenaries with no attachment to England travelled over and garrisoned castles in Stephen's name. In practice, the mercenaries operated independently, forcing the locals to supplement their pay and taking what they wanted with little or no consideration to Stephen's wishes. The confusion and turmoil in England can in part be seen by the coinage issued during this period. Silver coins were minted by the rival courts of Stephen and Matilda, but Stephen's eldest son Eustace also minted coins whilst governor of York and Earl Robert of Gloucester also minted his own silver coins. Silver coins were a necessity to pay for soldiers and the material of war; these were not particularly used for local exchange and purchases.

In 1147 the Empress Matilda suffered a serious blow to her hopes. Her main support Earl Robert of Gloucester died. Without Robert, Matilda was denied her primary military leader and faced defeat if she remained at the head of the faction that opposed King Stephen. In 1148, perhaps in acknowledgement of her own inability to defeat King Stephen, Matilda left England. Her eldest son Henry Fitz Empress would soon be sixteen. It was now time for him to oppose King Stephen.

Task: The Anarchy

Write a response to the following question;

"To what extent do you agree with the view that the main reason why King Stephen was able to continue to rule from 1135-1148 was due to the lack of a viable alternative?

Write your response in no more than 500 words

1.3 The early years of Henry 1133-1151

In this section we will;

- *Understand the circumstances of the birth and connections of the future King Henry II*
- *Explore the major events of Henry's early life*
- *Begin to consider the relationship between Henry and the English and French Kings*
- *Continue to investigate the period of civil war known as 'The Anarchy'*

What's in a name?

King Henry II is described in medieval sources and in modern history books alike by a variety of names and descriptions, a selection of which are as follows;

- King Henry II,
- Henry of Anjou
- Henry Plantagenet
- Henry FitzEmpress (sometimes written as 'fitzEmpress')
- Henry Curtmantle
- The Old King

All of these descriptions can be a little confusing. Some, like Henry Curtmantle were contemporary nicknames. Others, such as Henry Plantagenet were first coined in the 16th century. Some of these descriptions are in favour at some points and fall out of favour in subsequent years. None of these descriptions is necessarily incorrect and as you expand your knowledge and understanding of Henry's life and reign as King of England and ruler of the Angevin Empire (another term whose usage could be debated!) you will encounter many if not all of the descriptors used as stated above.

At various phases of the life of Henry it is perhaps appropriate to use one term that we shall no longer use later on. In this study guide we shall describe Henry as Henry FitzEmpress in the years before he is crowned King of England in 1154; as it is through his mother Matilda, the former empress of Germany that Henry pursued his claim to the crown of England. After Henry has been crowned King we shall call Henry by his principal title; King Henry II.

Plantagenet

The term 'Plantagenet' which is sometimes used to describe the dynasty of Kings of England from Henry II (1154-89) to Richard II (1377-1399).

These kings themselves however would not have recognised this term. Henry's father Geoffrey was known to wear on occasion a sprig of yellow blossom in his hats. This plant's latin name was 'planta genista', and it is from this habit by Henry's father that the term Plantagenet is used to describe the kingly descendants of Geoffrey of Anjou.

The birth of Henry and family links

Henry was the eldest son of Geoffrey Plantagenet, Count of Anjou and Matilda, daughter of King Henry I was born on the 5th March 1133 in the town of Le Mans in the County of Anjou.

Henry's first journey to England 1142-1144

> ***Henry 'Curtmantle'***
>
> *In your research of Henry II you may encounter the word 'Curtmantle'.*
>
> *A 'Curtmantle' was a fashionable style of short cloak that Henry often liked to wear.*

In November 1142, Henry, now aged nine, accompanied some 300 knights dispatched from Normandy and Anjou to England. These knights were sent to help the Empress Matilda in her struggle against King Stephen. Henry, still being a child, was of little practical assistance to his mother during the Anarchy, however Henry's very presence would have provided some moral support to his mother and presented an additional reason to justify the rebellion against King Stephen.

In actuality however, the real reason for the young Henry's arrival in England was for him to undergo education and exposure to the people and lands of England.

Henry went to Bristol and remained in the West Country for some fifteen months. Here he was raised in the household of his uncle, Robert, Earl of Gloucester. In 1144 Henry returned to the continent , probably to Anjou, where his education was continued under the tutorage of academics such as William of Conches. Henry also spent time in the company of his father and was able to observe how Geoffrey ruled his household and his lands.

Henry's invades England - 1147

In 1147 Henry, now aged thirteen, demonstrated something of his character and a streak of independence. He decided to invade England without the support of his father or mother. His father had by now completed the conquest of Normandy and had little or no thoughts for England. His mother, the Empress Matilda had recently decided to abandon the struggle for England and had left the country after her position deteriorated and the death of her brother and key supporter, Robert, Earl of Gloucester.

Henry, even now acquiring nicknames such as 'Curtmantle' had raised a small army of mercenaries and along with a tiny force of household knights, Henry FitzEmpress sailed for England.

Rumour exaggerated Henry's force into a great invasion and the expedition landed in Southern England in late 1147. No doubt Henry hoped and expected to gather his Mother's supporters together and continue the contest with King Stephen.

In fact, Henry's invasion was something of a farce. Henry received little or no support and after a few weeks of parading his tiny force around Wiltshire, Henry discovered that he could not afford to pay for the few hundred mercenaries he brought with him. The result was predictable. The Mercenaries deserted and Henry FitzEmpress was forced to retreat back across the Channel.

King Stephen could have tried to capture or even kill Henry. However he did no such thing. He certainly did not view Henry FitzEmpress as a real threat. Instead King Stephen rounded up Henry's former mercenaries and paid them the money they were owed before arranged their transportation back to the continent.

Lessons learned

For Henry FitzEmpress however, the experience was useful. Henry learned several hard lessons. He knew that his name alone was not enough to gather support against King Stephen. He lacked wealth and land with which to reward his supporters or to attract new ones. Henry also learned that professional mercenaries could be an effective military force, but that without wealth you could not hope to keep them in your service.

Henry's third visit to England - 1149

In 1149, Henry FitzEmpress returned to England. He was now aged sixteen and on the verge of adulthood. Henry announced himself during this period as;

'Henry, son of the daughter of King Henry I and rightful heir of England and Normandy'.

Despite this grand sound challenge to King Stephen, Henry did not attempt to repeat the mistakes of his last trip to England. Instead, Henry rode rapidly through England and travelled North to visit his Great Uncle, King David of Scotland. Here Henry FitzEmpress was formally knighted by King David at the town of Carlisle; a town at this point on the border between Scotland and England. Henry also made contact with Ranulf, Earl of Chester; the most powerful lord in Northern England and in rebellion from King Stephen since 1141.

Together, Henry and Ranulf led an army to attack the city of York. York was loyal to King Stephen and governed by his eldest son Eustace. The city was besieged, but only briefly. King Stephen, now taking Henry FitzEmpress seriously, led an army north to relieve the city. The siege was broken and Henry was forced to retreat all the way back to Normandy. He did however manage to prevent Eustace from capturing the town of Devizes, which was loyal to Henry and his mother Matilda.

Duke of Normandy

> ***A vow of Homage***
>
> *Below is a typical declaration of homage performed by a tenant for his lands;*
>
> *'I become your man for the tenement which I hold of you, and I will bear you fealty in life, limb and earthly honour'.*

In 1150, Geoffrey of Anjou formally granted his son Henry the title of Duke and the lands of Normandy. Henry however faced a new threat; that of the King of France.

King Louis VII of France had recently returned from the fiasco that was the Second Crusade. Whilst in Palestine Louis had encountered defeat and humiliation on the political stage, but had also determined to divorce his rather wayward wife, Eleanor of Aquitaine.

King Louis therefore was not inclined to accept a new Duke in Normandy that he did not approve of and who did not know his place. On hearing the Henry had become Duke of Normandy, King Louis declared instead that Eustace, the son of King Stephen was the rightful Duke and invaded Normandy.

Henry and his father responded to this aggressive act with diplomacy. In August 1151 Louis accepted the homage of Henry for the Duchy of Normandy in return for the surrender of the region called 'The Vexin'. This strategic region lay along the river Seine and bordered the lands of the French King with Normandy.

The family tree of King Henry II's ancestors

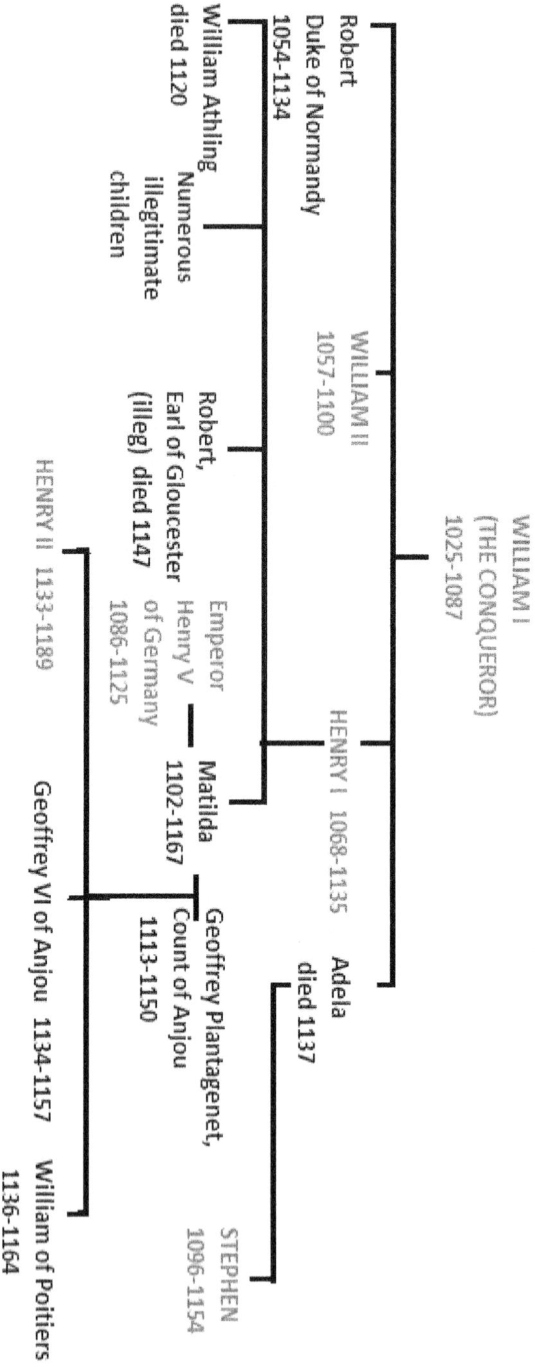
WILLIAM I
(THE CONQUEROR)
1025-1087
Robert
Duke of Normandy
1054-1134
WILLIAM II
1057-1100
HENRY I 1068-1135
Adela
died 1137
William Athling
died 1120
Numerous
illegitimate
children
Robert,
Earl of Gloucester
(illeg) died 1147
Emperor
Henry V
of Germany
1086-1125
Matilda
1102-1167
Geoffrey Plantagenet,
Count of Anjou
1113-1150
STEPHEN
1096-1154
HENRY II 1133-1189
Geoffrey VI of Anjou 1134-1157
William of Poitiers
1136-1164

Count of Anjou, Maine and Touraine

In September 1151, shortly after Henry had made his homage to King Louis VII for the Duchy of Normandy, his father Geoffrey of Anjou died of an illness aged only thirty nine.

Henry, now aged eighteen, as Count of Anjou, Maine and Touraine, was one of the largest landowners and powerful men in France. But this was not the limits of his power and authority. He would soon add the Duchy of Aquitaine to his possessions – extending his own power to a point where it potentially exceeded that of the King of France.

Henry's lands in 1150-1151

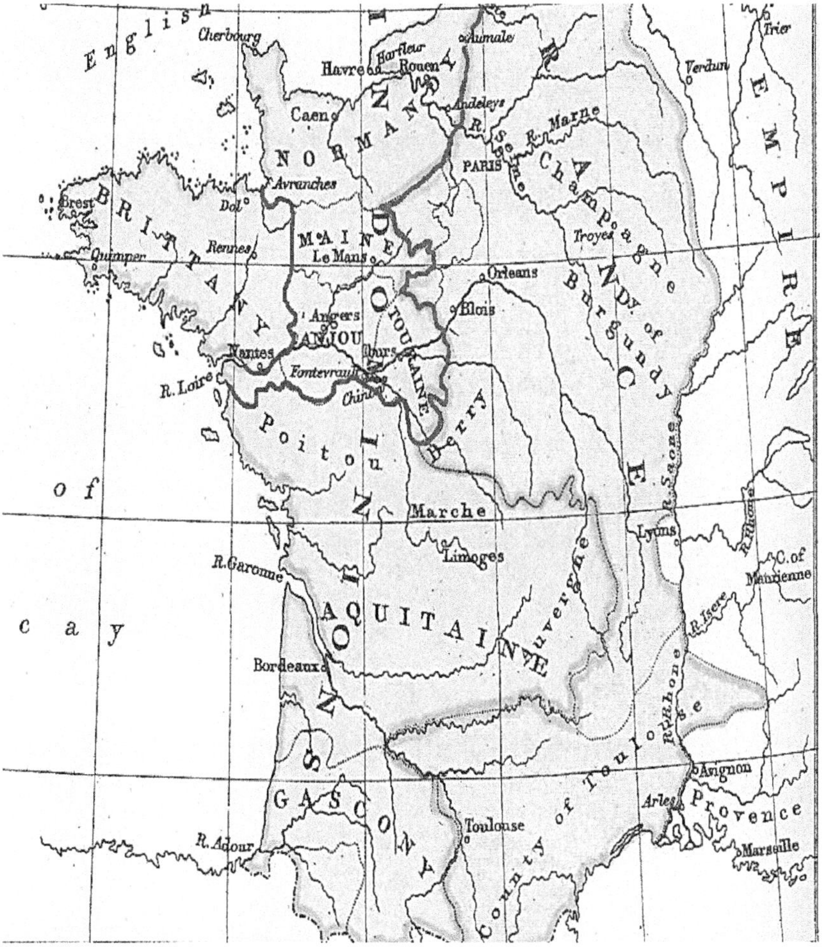

Task: Henry's early years

Write a short written response to the following question;

To what extent do you think that it was Henry's family connections that primarily resulted in his rapid rise to power?

Write your response in no more than 300 words

1.4 Henry and Eleanor of Aquitaine -1152

In this section we will;

- *Understand the importance of the Duchy of Aquitaine*
- *Explore the major events of Henry's early life*
- *Understand who Eleanor of Aquitaine was*
- *Begin to consider the relationship between Eleanor and Henry*
- *Begin to consider the relationship between Henry and the English and French Kings*

The Duchy of Aquitaine

The Duchy of Aquitaine was a large region of France. It covered more than a quarter of the total land area of France and occupied the South-western Quarter of the country. It included the towns of Bordeaux and Poitiers; the latter of which was the Ducal capital. Aquitaine encompassed several regions including the counties of Chateau-Roux, Gascony, Aunis, Poitiers, La Manche, Saintonge, Limousin, Perigord and Auvergne.

Potentially the duchy of Aquitaine was capable of delivering to its ruler's immense wealth. It occupied profitable routes of communication to Spain and controlled much of the Western sea board of France. Potentially the Duke of Aquitaine had strong links to the neighbouring territories of Barcelona and Navarre in the Spanish peninsula and Toulouse to the East.

Aquitaine was a distinct region of France not just politically, but also culturally. The inhabitants of Aquitaine had different styles in clothes and tastes in music and food. They also spoke a different dialect of French. In Aquitaine the inhabitants spoke *'langue d'oc'*, a Southern French dialect that today is more similar to Catalan than to French. In Northern France the inhabitants spoke *'langue d'oil'*, a precursor of modern French.

In practice, the Dukes of Aquitaine often struggled to maintain much authority over their lords and major vassals. Major landowners in Aquitaine were often effectively self-governing and regularly rebelled against their Duke.

In September 1151 at the time of Henry's accession to the Counties of Anjou, Maine and Touraine the Duchy of Aquitaine was ruled by

A Timeline of Henry's rapid acquisition of land and title

1149 Henry is landless with no official title

1150 Made Duke of Normandy by his Father

1151 (August) Henry swears homage to Louis VII of France for Normandy

1151 (September) Henry becomes Count of Anjou, Maine and Touraine

1152 (May) Henry marries Eleanor of Aquitaine; becomes Duke of Aquitaine

King Louis VII of France. King Louis VII possessed Aquitaine through his marriage to the rightful heir; the Duchess Eleanor of Aquitaine. This marriage however was due to end suddenly and soon.

Eleanor of Aquitaine

Eleanor of Aquitaine was born in 1122 and was therefore some nine years older than Henry FitzEmpress. In 1137, when Eleanor was aged fifteen, her father Duke William X died whilst on pilgrimage to Santiago de Compostela in North Western Spain. William had no sons and Eleanor was his eldest daughter. As a result, Eleanor became the rightful heir to the largest Duchy in France; but in addition to being female, she was also still a child.

Eleanor's first marriage took place in 1137. King Louis VI of France was eager to ensure that he would have control of Aquitaine. To accomplish this, Louis VI arranged a marriage between Eleanor and his seventeen year old son, also named Louis. Three months after the death of William X, the marriage took place in Bordeaux. Aquitaine was now under the control of the Kingdom of France. A few days after the wedding, Louis VI died. He was succeeded by his seventeen year old son, Louis VII; at his side was his new wife, Eleanor of Aquitaine, Queen of France.

The Queen of France

From the start it appears the marriage was a mismatch. Louis VII was religious and austere in his outlook. He liked to converse with monks and priests, prayed often and ate a simple meagre diet. Eleanor was extravagant. She liked the finest foods and the finest wines; she liked lavish entertainment, fanciful stories and dressed in the latest fashions.

Eleanor was also eager to involve herself in politics. Her sister Petronilla had an affair with a lord and Eleanor encouraged her husband to use this affair as an excuse to wage war on Petronilla's estranged husband.

In 1147, Eleanor insisted on accompanying her husband on the Second Crusade. She encouraged a group of women to train as soldiers to take part in the crusade. On arrival in Antioch, it was rumoured (probably falsely) that she had an affair with her Uncle, Raymond, Prince of Antioch. As a result Louis VII abandoned any cooperation with the Prince of Antioch and instead decided to attack Damascus. The Damascus campaign was a failure.

In 1148, on the way back from Jerusalem it was now clear that the marriage was in trouble. The Pope himself gave the royal couple some marriage counselling whilst they were in Rome.

Louis VII and Eleanor had two children together, born in 1145 and in 1150, but both were daughters and Louis desired a male heir to the throne. Soon after the birth of the second daughter, Louis VII took the step of having his marriage to Eleanor annulled. On the 21st March 1152 Louis VII used the often used and convenient excuse that the pair could not be married because they were too closely related. In doing so however, Louis VII had to surrender his authority over Aquitaine.

Eleanor and Henry

Eleanor was now once again the titular Duchess of Aquitaine. She was now once again the most desired bride in Western Europe. Many potential husbands were eager to marry Eleanor – whether she was willing or not.

Eleanor undertook a dangerous journey from the court of Louis VII, seeking safety back to Poitiers in her Duchy. Many lords and knights sought to locate and waylay her on the road, seize her and marry her. Potential suitors included the Count of Blois and Henry's own younger brother Geoffrey. But Eleanor managed to avoid them all.

Eleanor returned to Poitiers and almost immediately sent a message north to Henry FitzEmpress suggesting that the pair marry. Henry had first met Eleanor in 1151 when Henry had performed the act of homage for Normandy to Louis VII.

According to one contemporary the marriage proposal was desired by Henry;

"The duke indeed allured by the nobility of that woman and by desire for the great honours belonging to her, impatient at all delay, took with him a few companions, hastened quickly over the long routes and in little time obtained that marriage which he had long desired".

William of Newburgh

The couple married on the 18th May 1152 at Poitiers. Eleanor had been a single woman for some 58 days. In time the marriage would see many children. In all Henry and Eleanor would have eight children, five sons and three daughters. Their first son, William, would be born in 1153.

Henry had risen from a landless noble to ruler of over 50% of the landmass of the Kingdom of France in less than two years. As a result of his marriage to Eleanor, Henry was now Duke of Aquitaine as well as Duke of Normandy and Count of Anjou, Maine and Touraine. It was a meteoric rise.

Henry and Louis VII: the beginnings of enmity

Henry's meteoric rise to power and wealth had come swiftly, but he had made enemies along the way. King Stephen and his eldest son Eustace remained wary of Henry's next steps in England but it was King Louis VII of France who had the greatest motives to fear and hate Henry.

Louis VII had lost Aquitaine through his own actions, but he was angered that Henry (as a vassal, due to his act of homage) had not notified or asked for permission to marry the former Queen of France. Likewise, Eleanor also did not seek Louis VII's permission. Both technically should have done so and because they had not, Louis VII had lost face as the key authoritative figure in his own Kingdom. Louis VII saw Henry as a man of ambition. He had acquired vast land and great power in a short amount of time. He also had claims to pursue in England; where else might he decide to exert his own authority? Any further claims in France would impinge directly on the Kingdom of France and Louis VII's own rights and authority. The result was, according to Henry of Huntingdon *'great hatred and discord'*.

Henry's lands in 1152

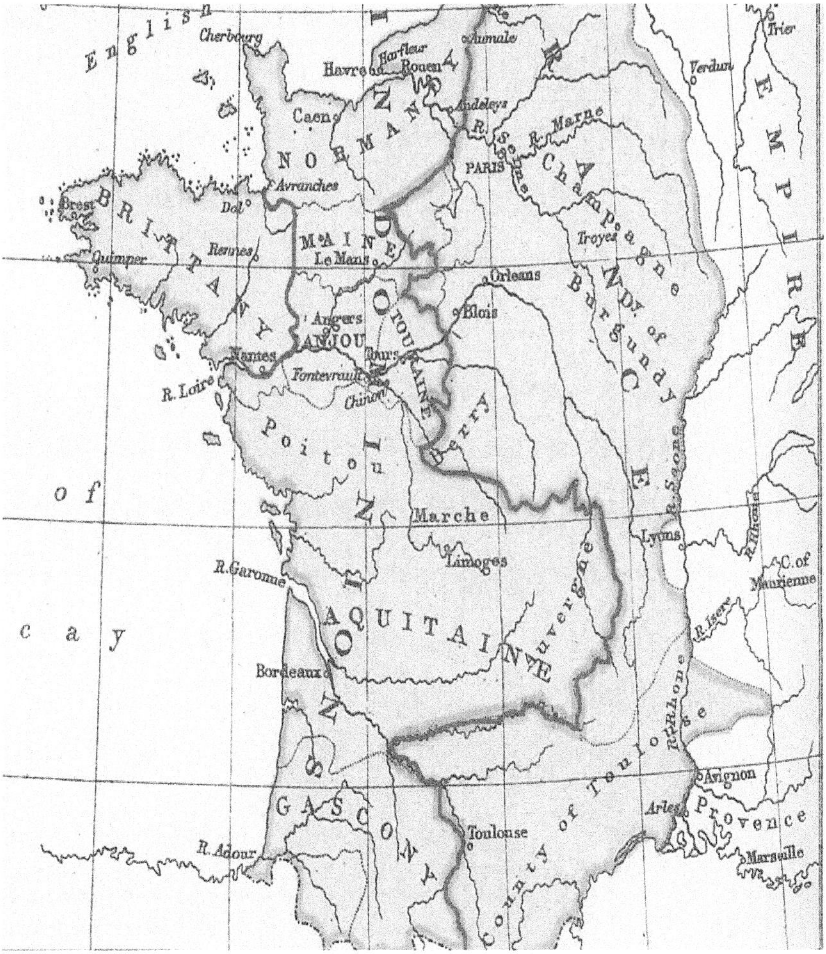

Task: Eleanor of Aquitaine

Research task

You may now find it helpful to conduct some research into Henry's wife; Eleanor of Aquitaine.

Using Internet search engines and your own access to books explore the life of Eleanor of Aquitaine.

Try to identify in particular;

- Her family tree
- Her children
- Her relationship with King Louis VII of France
- Her relationship with Henry II of England
- Her relationship with her sons; in particular Henry (the Young King), King Richard the Lionheart and King John.

Some websites you could use include;

www.bbc.co.uk/history/historic_figures/eleanor_of_aquitaine.shtml

www.history.com/topics/british-history/eleanor -of-aquitaine

Spend at least one hour in this task

Points for reflection;

- *Eleanor of Aquitaine spent much time in captivity; effectively imprisoned by her husband and her sons. Why do you think this happened?*
- *How influential do you think Eleanor of Aquitaine was on the major events of the period?*

1.5 Henry and Stephen 1153-1154

In this section we will;

- *Explore the major events of Henry's life*
- *Consider the importance of diplomacy in Medieval politics*
- *Understand King Stephen's relationship with the Barons and Earls of England*

The alliance against Henry FitzEmpress 1152

Henry FitzEmpress' rapid accession to power had not gone unnoticed. Those who stood to lose in the face of Henry's gain were encouraged to unite and work together to try and limit Henry's power.

The following lords united in 1152-3 against Henry FitzEmpress;

- King Louis VII of France
- King Stephen of England
- Eustace, Count of Boulogne (son of Stephen)
- Henry, Count of Champagne
- Robert, Count of Perche
- Geoffrey, Brother of Henry FitzEmpress

All of these men had reasons to attack Henry FitzEmpress. Some of these motives were very clear;

King Louis VII of France was angered by the marriage of Henry and Eleanor, and was jealous of the lands now under the authority of Henry; who was his vassal.

King Stephen saw in Henry a rival to himself for the throne of England. Count Eustace too, as King Stephen's eldest son stood to lose greatly if Henry deprived his father of the throne of England, as he saw himself as the rightful heir to England.

The Counts of Champagne and Perche were rulers of lands that neighboured Henry's own lands. They attacked Henry as it was they who could profit from taking land from Henry FitzEmpress.

For Geoffrey, Henry's brother the motives are a little less clear, however it is probable that he felt that he had been disinherited after the death of their father, Henry had after all taken all the titles and lands when his father died. Geoffrey perhaps hoped for the County of Anjou or at least a sizeable portion of the inheritance.

The course of events 1152

In the summer months of 1152 King Louis invaded the Duchy of Aquitaine whilst the Counts of Champagne and Perche invaded Normandy. In England King Stephen began to attack Henry's supporters in England and laid siege to the castle of Wallingford.

Henry therefore faced numerous threats in numerous places simultaneously. The manner of response would become typical for Henry, he moved swiftly and decisively against his opponents. He correctly identified which threats were most dangerous, and which were not, he also identified those which could be dealt with easily. Henry chose to ignore for the time being events in England. He could not risk crossing to England at this point. Instead Henry selected the threats that could be most easily dealt with first – the minor opposition.

Henry first dealt with the threat from the Counts of Champagne and Perche, stabilising the position and ensuring that they could not make easy progress. Geoffrey was then dealt with; a castle loyal to Geoffrey was taken and Geoffrey forced to surrender. Henry received a little bit of good fortune when King Louis VII fell ill and was forced to withdraw from active campaigning. A truce was made with Louis VII and the Counts of Champagne and Perche.

By the end of 1152 Henry could now turn his attention to England and King Stephen.

Henry invades England

In January 1153 Henry could now turn to England and attempt to deal with King Stephen once and for all. Henry left the bulk of his knights in Normandy, Anjou and Aquitaine and instead employed a force of several thousand mercenaries to accompany him to England. These mercenaries were well equipped, professional soldiers; men described in the *Gesta Stephani* as;

"men of the greatest cruelty"

Henry FitzEmpress might well be expected to go immediately to the assistance of the Castle of Wallingford – still under siege by King Stephen's men. Instead, Henry elected to conduct a siege of his own; he besieged the town of Malmesbury.

Henry managed to balance the situation in England. If King Stephen persisted in the siege of Wallingford, then he faced losing Malmesbury. The town held no real importance to King Stephen, but he was under pressure as a king to be able to demonstrate that he could govern and rule his kingdom. King Stephen abandoned his siege of Wallingford and marched with an army to confront Henry FitzEmpress.

Once the two armies came face to face, Henry elected not to begin a battle and King Stephen could not encourage his men to fight either. King Stephen had no option but to withdraw.

War-weariness

When Henry FitzEmpress invaded England in 1153, the barons and earls that comprised the core of King Stephen's armies had been involved in war and fighting to a greater or lesser extent since 1138.

The English barons and earls were largely dependent on their lands as their major source of wealth and these lands had been subject to war and devastation for over a decade. Many of these same men had lands in Normandy and for these lands they had to pay homage to Henry FitzEmpress, even if in England they were loyal to King Stephen. This conflict of interest ensured that now there was an established Duke of Normandy who was a viable alternative to King Stephen they were reluctant to fight a battle against the man who could strip them of their lands in Normandy.

The view seems to be that the nobles of England now loyal to King Stephen could see that only through some king of agreed settlement, a diplomatic solution, could there be any outcome which would see these men able to retain their lands on both sides of the English Channel. In practice, this meant that King Stephen would need to recognise Henry as the next King of England.

After the non-battle of Malmsbury, Henry undertook a campaign in the Midlands, moving rapidly, raiding and moving along. In doing so Henry demonstrated that he was an effective war leader to the Anglo-Norman Barons of England and that King Stephen was powerless to prevent him from conducting this raid. Barons began to desert King Stephen in favour of Henry. One key supporter to desert to Henry was Robert, Earl of Leicester and a noble who had been richly rewarded by King Stephen for many years.

Henry was seen more and more as the future and King Stephen the past. As Henry progressed through the Midlands he in turn realised that his mercenaries were increasingly seen as a barrier between him and the English lords. England was full of mercenaries in 1153 and they were feared for their rapaciousness and violence. Henry saw that his own mercenaries were little needed. Henry chose to dismiss some 500 of his own mercenaries and ship them back to their homes on the continent. However the English Channel could erupt in storms and many of these men died in shipwrecks.

The use of mercenaries by Henry

The decision to use mercenaries rather than the forces of his vassals was sensible. Knights could only be required to serve for a limited amount of time, they were expensive to maintain whilst in the field and also it would be very expensive to transport a large number of knights to England by ship. In comparison, mercenary infantry soldiers were more easily transportable. Mercenaries also served for pay, so long as you could pay them, they would remain in your service. Finally and perhaps most importantly, in England Henry could draw upon the knights of those lords loyal to him such as Earl Ranulf of Chester, mercenaries on the other hand were, as professional soldiers more experienced at siege warfare and, to put it bluntly, more expendable. If Henry failed then the loss of mercenaries would cost Henry nothing, the loss of a great lord, or large number of knights and lords would result in a host of other difficulties including redistribution of lands, inheritances and so forth.

The death of Eustace

In the summer of 1153 King Stephen tried one last time to fight Henry in battle. At the castle of Wallingford, which lay between London and Oxford, Henry brought his army to try and end the siege of Wallingford, whilst King Stephen led a new force out of London. However the two armies once again refused to fight. The soldiers and nobles that comprised these forces would not risk their lives in what they saw as a pointless fight. Both Stephen and Henry had no other choice but to try and seek a diplomatic solution.

At the urging of their barons and the English clergy, the two leaders met face to face at Wallingford and opened negotiations in August. One man refused to have any dealings with the peace now under discussion; Eustace, son of Stephen.

Eustace had the most to lose from any peace settlement that would see him effectively lose the crown of England in the future. Eustace stormed away to conduct raids and pillaging in the West of England, however he soon took sick and within days he had died, aged twenty-three. It may have been a sickness such as dysentery which was fairly common and sometimes fatal, perhaps it was poison. In any event, for Henry FitzEmpress, Eustace's death was certainly convenient. King Stephen was devastated by the loss of his eldest son and heir, but this grief did not prevent him from coming to a formal peace with Henry that suited them both.

What's in a name?

The Peace between Henry and Stephen is known by a variety of names.

It is sometimes called the Treaty of Wallingford (where it was first agreed), the Treaty of Winchester and the Treaty of Westminster (both locations were the treaty was pronounced after it had been ratified in the presence of assembled barons, earls and clergymen).

Peace

In November 1153 King Stephen and Henry FitzEmpress formally agreed to make peace and end the civil war in England. King Stephen was now aged 61, Henry was 20. In the full audience of the assembled barons and earls of England Henry gave homage to King Stephen and was recognised as his heir. King Stephen's son William then gave homage to Henry for his lands.

For the barons this peace meant that the Barons could finally look to ruling their lands in both England and Normandy without fearing for their safety. The treaty was formally ratified at Westminster in December 1153 but was variously known as the Peace of Wallingford, Winchester or Westminster as both Stephen and Henry went on a joint tour that presented to their subjects that the peace was genuine, made between equals and that England could look forward to the hope of times of prosperity.

The Treaty of Westminster 1154

The Treaty of Westminster was ratified in December 1154. The Treaty ended the period of civil war in England known and the main points of the Treaty were as follows;

- King Stephen was to remain as King with full royal authority until his death.
- King Stephen would recognise Henry FitzEmpress as his heir.
- King Stephen would listen to any advice Henry gave.
- William, the son of King Stephen would renounce any future claim to the throne of England in return for substantial land rights and title.
- Henry would take possession of several royal castles in England and be responsible for the upkeep of the men who manned them. King Stephen was to have full access to these castles at any time.
- All foreign mercenaries in England were to be disbanded and returned to their homes.

The death of King Stephen – October 1154

In March 1154 Henry left England to help King Louis VII of France subdue a rebellion in the Vexin. King Stephen continued to travel around England and began to implement some of the strategies agreed by himself and Henry, including reordering and establishing the coinage of England.

King Stephen however was an ill man, and on the 25th October 1154, King Stephen died. He was buried at the monastery of Faversham (which no longer exists).

King Stephen and the English Barons

King Stephen had been a major baron and landowner in England under King Henry I (1100-1135) and a favourite of that King. As such he was seen by the barons and earls of England as one of them; a peer of the realm.

When Stephen moved to seize the throne of England in 1135 he was able to succeed in part because he was familiar whereas Empress Matilda was a stranger and he was also able to secure his kingship because he was personable. He knew how to appeal to people and to get them to support him. Even hostile sources acknowledged that

King Stephen was approachable, gentle and possessed a good sense of humour.

However, King Stephen knew that to encourage support and good feeling towards himself among the barons and earls of England he needed to possess more than a good nature, he encouraged his supporters with generous rewards of lands and titles. However, his ability to reward land and title was finite and when he would not or could not reward barons and earls appropriately they could seek to support his rival the Empress Matilda and later her son FitzEmpress.

King Stephen for example rewarded followers like the Waleran brothers with huge grants of land in the Midlands, but denied these same rewards to men like the Earls of Gloucester and Chester. Each major lord also had a set of individual rights and agreements with King Stephen as part of the terms of their tenancies of lands. The result was then that barons felt that their neighbours might have better lands or terms of service than they themselves. This caused some resentment and motives to support Stephen's rival.

English Earls

The result of King Stephen's policies was to grant away royal lands to barons and earls and the creation of a number of new earldoms. By the time of King Stephen's death there were twenty three Earls in England. Previously they had numbered around a dozen. Each Earl had an individual relationship and demands of service to the King.

English Earls were the equivalent of French Counts in rank and the title indicated a man of high noble status. Earls possessed large areas of lands; however these lands were usually in various areas across England and did not necessarily match established county lands. Earl Ranulf for example was Earl of Chester but possessed lands and interests in the Midlands and in Lincolnshire. Furthermore, earldoms were not necessarily hereditary and the sons and heirs of earls might not have their father's lands passed on to them by the King.

Other questions that concerned Earls were the level of obligations that they were required to give to their king. How much per year were they liable to pay to the King? How many knights and soldiers were they obliged to provide for service under the King? And were these knights and soldiers required to serve in other lands and for how long? The answers to these questions varied between Earls and was a potential source of much confusion, jealously and resentment.

Task: The importance of diplomacy

Consider the following question;

"To what extent do you agree with the view that a diplomatic solution to end 'The Anarchy' was the best outcome for Henry fitzEmpress in 1153?"

Consider the following points and address each of the following points with 1-2 paragraphs;

- Henry's continued obligations and responsibilities elsewhere.
- The fortunes of Empress Matilda in confronting Stephen.
- The aims and hopes of the barons and earls of England.
- King Stephen's position.
- The state of England in 'The Anarchy'

Also write no more than 2 paragraphs that conclude and summarise your own view on the points raised.

Spend at least one hour in this task

The Counties of England at the time of Henry II

Part Two: King Henry II: The early years 1154-1172

PART TWO: King Henry II: the early years 1154-72

2.1 Henry II, King of England 1154

In this section we will;

- *Explore what the sources tell us about King Henry II's physical description and personality*
- *Begin to explore the medieval source material that deals with Henry II*

Introduction

When Henry FitzEmpress heard the news that King Stephen of England had fallen ill and subsequently died on the 25th October 1154, Henry was in Normandy.

Henry had been in Normandy since March 1154, helping King Louis VII of France to subdue a revolt in the Vexin; an important border region on the eastern edge of the Duchy of Normandy.

Henry returned to England as soon as he was able and made preparations for his coronation. On the 19th December 1154 at Westminster Abbey Henry was crowned king of the English. He was twenty one years old and already one of the most powerful men in Western Europe. His wealth and territory exceeded that of King Louis VII of France – who was technically Henry's overlord for much of his land.

A hope for England at the start of Henry II's reign

"England, long numbed by mortal chill, now you grow warm, revived by the heat of a new sun. You raise the country's bowed head, and with tears of sorrow wiped away, you weep for joy…With tears you utter these words to your foster child: 'You are spirit. I am flesh: now as you enter, I am restored to life".

Henry of Huntingdon

A drawing of Henry II

Below is a drawing from a contemporary manuscript. It depicts Henry II as the newly crowned monarch of England.

A drawing of Henry II

How do you think Henry II is portrayed in this drawing? Is he warlike? Peaceful? What is he holding and why might this be significant?

What was King Henry II like?

Medieval sources have left us with descriptions of King Henry II, both of his physical description, but some information regarding his personality. On the next several pages are some excerpts from some of these medieval writers describing King Henry II.

A Pen Portrait of the King

"Henry II was a man of reddish, freckled complexion, with a large, round head, grey eyes that glowed fiercely and grew bloodshot in anger, a fiery countenance and a harsh, cracked voice. His neck was thrust forward slightly from his shoulders, his chest was broad and square, his arms strong and powerful. His body was stocky, with a pronounced tendency towards fatness, due to nature rather than self-indulgence – which he tempered with exercise. For in eating and drinking he was moderate and sparing..."

"He was addicted to the chase beyond measure; at crack of dawn he was often on horseback, traversing wastelands, penetrating forests and climbing the mountain-tops, and so he passed restless days. At evening on his return home he was rarely to be seen to sit down, either before or after supper...he would wear the whole court out by continual standing..."

"He was a man of easy access, and condescending, pliant and witty, second to none in politeness....strenuous in warfare...very prudent in civil life...He was fierce towards those who remained untamed, but merciful towards the vanquished, harsh to his servants, expansive towards strangers, prodigal in public, thrifty in private...He was most diligent in guarding and maintaining peace, liberal beyond comparison in almsgiving and the peculiar defender of the Holy Land; a lover of humility, an oppressor of nobility and a contemner of the proud".

Gerald of Wales Book I, Chapter 46

Another pen portrait of the King;

...he was red-haired; however you will know that the lord king has been red-haired so far, except that the coming of old age and gray hair has altered that colour somewhat. His height is medium, so that neither does he appear great among the small, nor yet does he seem small among the great. His head is round, just as if the seat of great wisdom, and specially a shrine of lofty counsel. Such is the size of his head, that so it matches with his neck and with the whole body in proportionate moderation. His eyes are round, and white and plain, while he is of calm spirit; but in anger and disorder of heart they shine like fire and flash in fury. His hair is not in fear of the losses of baldness, nevertheless on top there is a tonsure of hairs; his leonine face is rather square. The eminence of his nose is weighed to the beauty of the whole body with natural moderation; curved legs, a horseman's shins, broad chest, and a boxer's arms all announce him as a man strong, agile and bold; nevertheless, in a certain joint of his foot the part of the toenail is grown into the flesh of his foot, to the vehement outrage of the whole foot. His hands testify grossly to the same neglect of his men; truly he neglects their care all the time; nor at any time, unless carrying birds, does he use gloves.

Peter of Blois: (excerpts from a letter to Walter, the archbishop of Palermo, in 1177)

Whom once he has esteemed, with difficulty he unloves them; whom once he has hated, with difficulty he receives into the grace of his familiarity. Always are in his hands bow, sword, spear and arrow, unless he be in council or in books. As often as he is able to rest from cares and anxieties, he occupies himself by reading alone, or in a crowd of clerics he labours to untangle some knot of inquiry...

Peter of Blois: (excerpts from a letter to Walter, the archbishop of Palermo, in 1177)

On his energy

Daily in mass, in counsels and in other public doings of the realm always from morning until vespers he stands on his feet. He never sits, unless riding a horse or eating, although he has shins greatly wounded and bruised with frequent blows of horses' hooves. In a single day, if necessary, he can run through four or five day-marches and, thus foiling the plots of his enemies, frequently mocks their plots with surprise sudden arrivals; he wears boots without a fold, caps without decoration, light apparel. He is a passionate lover of woods; while not engaged in battles, he occupies himself with birds and dogs. For in fact his flesh would weigh him down enormously with a great burden of fat, if he did not subdue the insolence of his belly with fasts and exercise; and also in getting onto a horse, preserving the lightness of youth, he fatigues almost every day the most powerful for the labour. Truly he does not, like other kings, linger in his palace, but traveling through the provinces he investigates the doings of all, judging powerfully those whom he has made judges of others. No one is more cunning in counsel, more fiery in speech, more secure in the midst of dangers, more cautious in fortune, more constant in adversity.

Peter of Blois: (excerpts from a letter to Walter, the archbishop of Palermo, in 1177)

Task: King Henry II

What sort of person do you think King Henry II was like?

Having read the pen portraits provided above, If you had to use 5 words to describe King Henry II – what 5 words would you use?

Consider if you think King Henry II might have been a likeable and popular figure based on these pen portraits.

2.2 Asserting the power of the King 1154-1160: England

In this section we will;

- *Continue to explore the medieval source material that deals with Henry II*
- *Consider what England was like during Henry II's reign*
- *Understand the difference between being 'King of England' and 'King of the English'*
- *Begin to consider the methods by which Henry II would rule*
- *Begin to consider the relationship between Henry II and Louis VII*
- *Explore the successes and failures of Henry II in the years 1154-1160*

Introduction

When Henry became King of England in 1154 he had a problem greater than any of his predecessors on the English throne. How could he effectively rule his vast domains?

Henry II and England at the beginning of his reign

When King Henry II was crowned on the 19th December 1154 at Westminster, he had with him his infant son William (unfortunately soon to take ill and die) and his heavily pregnant wife Eleanor of Aquitaine. Henry II was twenty one years of age and determined to put right England and help it to recover from the long period of civil war it had just emerged from.

Henry's Coronation Charter

Henry followed tradition by issuing a coronation charter. A Coronation Charter was a statement of intent – the King was giving notice on how they planned to rule.

King Henry II pledged in his coronation charter to grant to the earls and barons of England *'all the concessions, gifts, liberties and freedoms'* that they had enjoyed under the reign of King Henry I (1100-1135), Like Henry I, Henry II also pledged to abolish the 'evil customs' in the land and declared his desire to restore *'my whole realm'*.

By relating back to the reign of King Henry I, rather than King Stephen, in effect the new King was putting his English subjects on notice that the acts of his immediate predecessor could now be declared as invalid and illegal. Lords who had been granted land and favour by King Stephen could now face losing all that they had gained.

King Henry II also broke from tradition by having himself crowned as *'King of England'* rather than *'King of the English'*. The Anglo-Saxon rulers or England and the Norman kings that had replaced them had all continued to declare themselves *'Kings of the English'*.

Task: King of England vs King of the English

Write a brief response to the following question;

Why do you think King Henry II insisted on being crowned *'King of England'* rather than the traditional *'King of the English'?*

Write your response in no more than 10 minutes

The state of England in 1154: Henry II's four major challenges

Henry II came to the kingship of England and was faced with an England in a state of disorder and turmoil.

King Stephen had granted much royal land away to his supporters throughout his reign. As a result of measures such as this and also because of the civil war, the income received by the exchequer of England had effectively halved by 1154.

King Stephen had also extended the number of Earls in England. Previously there had been around a dozen Earls in England, by 1154 there were twenty three.

The northern counties had been attacked and occupied either by the Scottish king, or by Earls who now saw themselves as effectively independent. Finally, another problem faced by King Henry II was the proliferation of illegal castles.

Henry II asserts his authority on the nobles

Illegal/ Adulterine Castles

Illegal Castles were also called 'Adulterine' castles – a term we also associate today with adultery – to have an unauthorised relationship with someone other than a marriage partner.

Henry II's coronation charter was soon followed by the order that all lands, towns and castles that had formerly belonged to King Henry I (1100-1135) that had been granted away by King Stephen (1135-1154).

In practice many nobles that freely returned these properties had much of this property restored to them by King Henry II. In doing so Henry II was demonstrating that it was he who was in charge; that he possessed royal authority and that it was from him that the earls and barons of England would need to rely for their continued prosperity. Those barons and earls that possessed lands in both England and Normandy were easier to control. If they resisted Henry; they could face losing lands on both sides of the English Channel.

Illegal castles

Motte- and- Bailey Castle

A simple design for a castle that can be constructed rapidly in order to control a local region. Motte-and-Bailey castles were usually constructed out of wood.

It comprises a 'Motte' which was a mound of earth atop a tower or keep often constructed of wood or stone. The 'Bailey' was an enclosed area, a walled area that surrounded the Motte.

Perhaps one hundred illegal castles were taken and destroyed by King Henry II. Most of these castles were humble affairs, wooden stockades, with a wooden tower surrounded by a ditch. These motte and bailey castles had sprung up during the Anarchy and now that the civil war had ended, these castles were seen as an impediment to stable and peaceful rule.

An example of an illegal castle has been identified by archaeologists at Hamstead Marshall (Newbury Castle). This illegal castle was constructed by John Marshall, the father of William Marshall in 1152 and demolished soon after Henry II became king. It was a Motte and Bailey castle constructed out of wood with a ditch surrounding it.

Resistance in England 1155-1156

Not every Baron and Earl was happy with King Henry II exerting his authority in this way. Therefore Henry II decided to demonstrate that if necessary his bite was much worse than his bark. Henry II gathered together a large army and began a parade around England prepared to expel any baron who might try to disobey him. Several did.

Roger of Hereford

Roger of Hereford was a baron who had lands along the Welsh border. At first Roger was reluctant to surrender several illegal castles that he had constructed. However, he was convinced to surrender these places through a mediated surrender by Gilbert Foliot, the Bishop of Hereford.

Hugh de Mortimer

Hugh de Mortimer, a baron with lands along the Welsh border and in Staffordshire was one such baron. He had several castles including at Wigmore and Bridgenorth. Henry II besieged Bridgenorth castle for several weeks and nearly lost his life at this siege. An archer on the castle walls fired at King Henry II who was saved by the intervention of one of his knights; Hubert de St.Clair, who took the arrow in the chest and subsequently died. Hugh de Mortimer was eventually forced to surrender, but upon surrendering Hugh was permitted to retain his lands and three castles. Hugh was an important landowner along the Welsh Border and it was perhaps this necessary requirement for strong lordship along the Welsh border that helped persuade Henry II to retain him in his position.

Henry of Blois

Henry of Blois, the Bishop of Winchester and brother of King Stephen possessed six castles. He was forced to surrender these castles and went into exile. Perhaps the Bishop of Winchester was too closely associated with the former regime to be permitted to remain in post, but the Church as a landowner had profited under King Stephen and King Henry II was eager to make steps to restrict the authority of the Church in England. The bishop of Winchester's castles were destroyed.

William of Aumerle

William of Aumerle, a baron in North Yorkshire was another lord reluctant to surrender to the authority of King Henry II. He held a castle of Scarborough which Henry II seized control of and rebuilt.

Task: Resistance in England?

Why was resistance to Henry II limited in England in 1154-1155?

Rank the following factors in order of importance;

- Lack of a viable alternative
- Exhaustion after the Anarchy
- Henry's own military power
- Henry's use of clemency and diplomacy

Write a brief explanation for your choice, you should spend no more than 20 minutes on this activity.

2.3 Asserting the power of the King 1154-1160: Europe

In this section we will;

- *Continue to explore the medieval source material that deals with Henry II*
- *Begin to consider the methods by which Henry II would rule*
- *Begin to consider the relationship between Henry II and Louis VII*
- *Explore the successes and failures of Henry II in the years 1154-1160*

Introduction

When Henry became King of England in 1154 he had a problem greater than any of his predecessors on the English throne. How could he effectively rule his vast domains both in England and in France?

Henry II and his lands in France at the beginning of his reign

When King Henry II became King of England he was already lord of large amounts of land in Europe. Henry II himself was not English; he was born in Anjou in modern central France. Although England required a large amount of attention in the 1150s, Henry II also needed to keep his attention on his lands on the continent where he was faced with other problems and challenges.

The lands ruled by Henry II in 1154

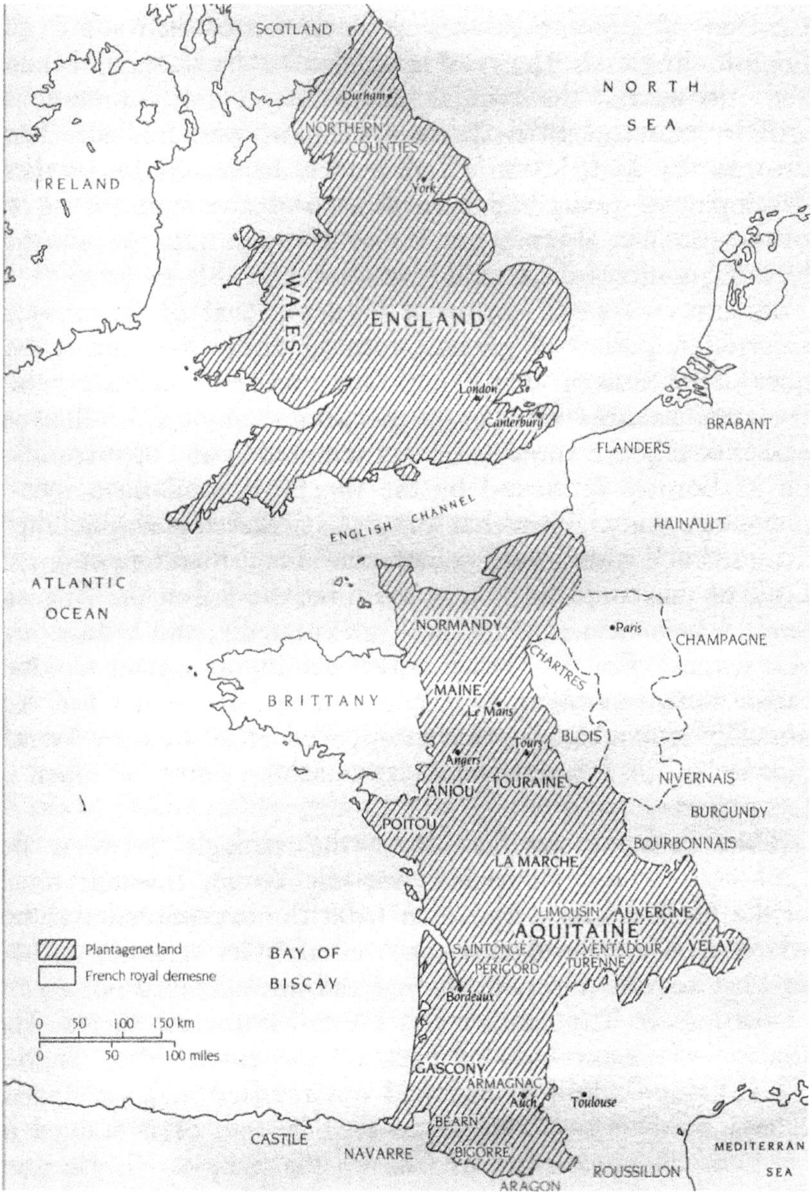

Rebellion in Anjou 1156

In 1156 King Henry II had to hurry back to his continental lands in order to face down another potential threat.

Henry II had two younger brothers; Geoffrey and William. It may have been that when Henry's father died in 1151 his Will may have indicated that his father desired for Geoffrey and William to share in the inheritance that Henry II had seized in full.

King Henry II returned to the Continent in the winter of 1155/6. In January 1156, Henry II gave homage once again to King Louis VII of France for his Duchies of Normandy and Aquitaine and the Counties of Anjou, Maine and Touraine. This move was wise as by giving homage to Louis VII for these lands, it would now be difficult for Louis VII to side with Henry's brothers and support their claims.

Henry II, armed with this support, then met his brothers at Rouen in February 1156 at a meeting arranged by their mother Matilda and at this meeting Henry II must have made clear to Geoffrey in no uncertain terms that he was not willing to share the inheritance of their father. Henry II had also been in communication with the Pope and was provided with a document from the leading churchman of Europe that gave him permission to ignore his father's Will.

Geoffrey however was not content with this decision. He rebelled and seized several castles in Anjou and along the Normandy border. Henry II had however brought some of his forces from England and these men were put to work in stamping out the rebellion.

By the end of 1156, Geoffrey had been forced to surrender. He renounced all claim to the County of Anjou in return for a cash pension of 1000 English pounds and possession of a castle at Loudon in Anjou. Shortly after, some good news reached Geoffrey. He had been elected as Count of Brittany; the region lying to the West of Normandy.

Geoffrey did not long remain as Count however, he died in 1158; still in early twenties and since he was without children, his brother Henry II now had a claim to the County of Brittany, which he was not slow to claim.

King Henry and King Malcolm IV, 1157

In 1157 Henry II was back in England and inspecting the northern regions of the country. At Peveril Castle King Henry II arranged a meeting with King Malcolm IV of Scotland and relations between the two kings were formalised.

The Scottish kings had invaded England during the Anarchy and despite being defeated in 1138 at the battle of the Standard, had effectively asserted their authority over the northern counties of Northumbria and Cumbria. Now, faced with King Henry II and the substantial army that he brought with him, King Malcolm formally relinquished his claims to these regions and received in return the Earldom of Huntingdon – a title and properties in the midlands that had previously been granted to the kings of Scotland.

King Henry and the Welsh 1157

King Henry II had brought an army to England for a reason. Not only had he used this force to help persuade the King of Scotland to respect the northern frontier, Henry II was determined to deal with the Welsh.

The Welsh had been nominally independent of England previously, however Welsh princes and the Anglo-Norman barons who owned land along the border between Wales and England had often indulged in localised warfare. As a result towns such as Chester and Chepstow were often subject to attacks and were well defended with walls and castles as a result.

The Anarchy and the reign of King Stephen had provided the Welsh princes with some good opportunities to raid and profit from the distraction afforded. Henry II was determined to overawe the Welsh in turn.

Two Welsh princes in particular were hostile to Henry II; Owain Gwynedd and Rhys ap Gruffydd of Deheubarth. Henry II entered the mountainous territory of North Wales and almost met his death in an ambush at Ewloe Wood, also known as Coleshill. One Earl accompanying the King, the Earl of Essex fled the battle and was later stripped of his lands and title for this cowardice.

Henry II managed to continue his campaign and reached the coastline facing Ireland. As he progressed he constructed castles and took hostages.

The Welsh princes did agree to a peace with Henry II were they recognised his authority. In return, Henry II was allowed to recruit Welsh fighting men as mercenaries to serve in his army. As soldiers these men were known for their skill with both spear and with longbows.

Henry and Brittany 1158

In 1158, King Henry II was back on the continent. His brother Geoffrey had been appointed Count of Brittany, however he had died after only being Count for just over a year, the new Count was a Breton named Conan who also possessed lands in Yorkshire in England and the title the Earl of Richmond. As such he was a vassal of Henry II. Conan's lands and titles in England were confiscated.

Conan and the Bretons were reluctant to recognise Henry II as their overlord and instead looked to King Louis VII of France. Henry II combined diplomatic pressure with a demonstration of his military might.

The army he had used in England in 1157 was brought over to the continent, reinforced with Welsh mercenaries as well as mercenaries from Flanders and put to work in laying siege to the towns and castles of Brittany. Nantes was besieged and forced to recognise his authority.

Henry's son, the newborn Geoffrey was betrothed to Conan's five year old daughter. Conan was recognised as Count of Brittany for the remainder of his life so long as Geoffrey succeeded him.

Henry II was still eager to maintain good relations with King Louis VII. A large embassy was sent under Thomas Becket to the King at Paris and in 1158 it was agreed that Henry's infant son Henry was betrothed to the daughter of Louis VII, Margaret. The dowry of Margaret was agreed to be the Vexin; that sensitive region the lay on the eastern border of Normandy.

The siege of Toulouse 1159

Henry II was not yet finished in trying to assert his authority beyond his immediate borders. He had started this in 1157 on the English northern border, the Welsh frontier, Brittany and now in the south.

Toulouse was a wealthy County to the East of Aquitaine. The ruler of Toulouse was Count Raymond V, a distant relation of Queen Eleanor and a theoretical tenant of King Louis VII. Count Raymond V was however a nominally independent ruler, following in the footsteps of his illustrious ancestor, Raymond of St.Gilles who had been one of the leading Princes of the First Crusade.

For Henry II, Count Raymond V's semi-independent position was something that could be exploited. Perhaps a show of force would bring the County of Toulouse into Henry II's Angevin Empire.

Henry II raised £9000 from England to spend on his army. This sum was large; estimated at between 50-75% of the English exchequer in 1159. King Malcolm IV of Scotland sailed to join Henry II with a small army and Henry was even joined by the Count of Barcelona. Henry's tenants in chief joined him in force also; Chancellor Thomas Beckett had a retinue of 700 men.

For three months, from June-September 1159, Henry II's army besieged Toulouse. Toulouse was strongly defended and could hold out for some time, however Henry's army was large and well equipped with siege engines.

Henry II however did not calculate on the intervention of King Louis VII. Count Raymond called upon Louis to help his against this act of aggression and Louis hurried to help. He managed to gain entry to the city of Toulouse and present himself on the walls standing shoulder to shoulder with Count Raymond.

Henry and Louis 1159-1160

Henry II was now in a difficult position. If he continued the attack, he would be risking the life of the French king, who was his overlord for his lands of Anjou, Normandy and Aquitaine. This would result in war all along Henry's long frontier in France and also encourage his own lords in these lands to rebel. A long war on the continent may also result in rebellions in England. Louis too had raised an army and this force was on its way to Toulouse. Henry could be trapped against the walls of the city by this relieving force.

For Henry II the risk was too great. He broke off the siege and returned to his own lands. However he received an unexpected windfall on the return journey. King Stephen's last son, William died. William had been Count of Boulogne and held sizeable lands Normandy and in England. These lands now lacked a lord and were returned to King Henry II.

A short war nevertheless broke out between Henry and Louis, with most of the fighting on the Normandy border. Peace was made in 1160 when it was agreed that Henry's son and heir, the infant Henry would make homage to King Louis VII for Normandy.

The peace of 1160 lasted only briefly, Louis VII's second wife Constance died and Louis arranged a new marriage with Adelais of Blois; a niece of King Stephen and daughter of the Count of Blois. This new marriage potentially endangered the delicate balance between Henry II and Louis VII, and so Henry II moved to have the marriage between his son Henry and Margaret performed. Having done so, Henry II took control of Margaret's dowry and the Vexin was once again returned to Normandy. Louis VII responded with attacks on the region through 1160. This war ended only with the intervention of the Pope.

Task: Henry II's military expeditions 1154-1160

Write a response to the following question;

According to the historian Dan Jones; Henry was not so much leading a war of conquest as a war of recognition. To what extent do you agree with this view of Henry II's activities from 1154-1160?

Write your response in no more than 750 words.

2.4 Thomas Becket

In this section we will;

- *Explore the medieval source material that deals with Thomas Becket*
- *Understand the initial relationship between Henry II and Thomas Becket*
- *Explore the Constitutions of Clarendon*
- *Understand the reasons why this relationship deteriorated*

Introduction

When Henry became King of England in 1154 he had needed people to help him rule. Henry II relied on chosen men for positions like Justiciar, Treasurer, Chancellor and Chamberlain. He also needed good relationships with the Church and the Pope. We turn now to Thomas Becket; a man on whom Henry relied greatly during the early years of his reign and whose bloody demise marked a turning point in the reign of the king.

Henry and Archbishop Becket

The early life of Becket

Thomas Becket was born around 1118, the son of Gilbert Becket, a merchant from Rouen. Thomas grew up near London.

In his youth, Thomas Becket entered into the service of Theobald, the Archbishop of Canterbury. Becket became a deacon and then an archdeacon in his twenties. During the Anarchy, Becket was sent to Rome as part of an embassy from Archbishop Theobald to the Pope in order to obtain from the Pope permission to refuse King Stephen's wish to have his son Eustace crowned as *'Rex designatus'*. This mission was a success and Eustace was never recognised as the heir to the throne of England.

Archbishop Theobald was increasingly reliant upon Becket for the day to day administration of his affairs in Canterbury, therefore Becket acquired a sound understanding of the needs and requirements of the Church, but he had not become a priest.

By 1155 Becket had been introduced to King Henry II and evidently the pair got along well. Becket joined the *Curia Regis* and by 1156 had been appointed Henry II's Chancellor. With the command of the Chancellery, Becket had a high position; but his humble background meant that he had little income that did not derive directly from his position.

Unlike the Anglo-Norman baronial class that occupied many positions around the King, Becket was dependent upon the goodwill of his superiors for his financial security. As Chancellor to Henry II he was granted the stewardship of the Tower of London and also the castles of the Eye and Berkhampstead.

Key terms:

Deacon

A servant of the Church. A Deacon is a lay person or servant who serves the church without becoming a priest. They often served in administrative roles but could assist or even lead in some church services.

Archdeacon

An Archdeacon is a senior deacon and could serve as a representative of a Bishop or Archbishop.

'Rex designatus'

A recognized heir to the throne that has undergone a ceremonial crowning.

In England only the Archbishop of Canterbury had the authority to crown a king

Becket the Chancellor

Becket demonstrated his ability as Chancellor to Henry II. He entered the social circles of the barons and courted their favour and support, not just for himself, but also on behalf of Henry II. Becket ensured that the Church properties did not escape the raising of *scutage* 'Shield tax' and as a result of this effort; Becket ensured that additional funds entered the exchequer. It was through Becket's efforts that the £9000 raised to pay for Henry II's army that marched on Toulouse in 1159.

In 1158, Becket headed an embassy sent to King Louis VII of France at Paris. One contemporary source records the lavishness of this embassy;

"In his company he had some two hundred horsemen, knights, clerks, stewards and men in waiting, men at arms and squires of noble family, all in ordered ranks. All these and all their followers wore bright new festal garments...

Hounds and hawks were in the train...and eight five-horse chariots drawn by shire horses. On every horse was a sturdy groom in a new tunic, and on every chariot a warden. Two carts carried nothing but beer...for the French, who are not familiar with the brew, a healthy drink, clear, dark as wine, and finer in flavour...

He had twelve sumpter horses and eight chests of table places, gold and silver...One horse carried the plate, the altar furnishings and the books of his chapel...Every horse had a groom in a smart turn-out; every chariot had a fierce great mastiff on a leash standing in the cart or walking behind it, and every sumpter beast had a long tailed monkey on its back...

...there were about 250 men marching six or ten abreast, singing as they went in the English fashion. At intervals came braces of stag hounds and greyhounds and their attendants...then the men at arms, with the shields and chargers of the knights, then the other men at arms and boys and men bearing hawks...Last of all came the Chancellor and his friends."

Secretary to Becket; William FitzStephen

In 1159 Becket led a division of the army that marched on Toulouse. He possessed a personal retinue of some 700 knights and men at arms.

Becket as Chancellor maintained a lavish lifestyle. He entertained barons and notables with expensive banquets, entertainments and gifts. His relationship with Henry II seems to have been good; however Henry II did on occasion tease, even bully Becket. Henry II delighted in annoying Becket by riding into his banquets on a horse unannounced and forcibly stripped his Chancellor of his expensive cloak in order to give it to a poor old man they encountered in London.

In 1161 Archbishop Theobald died. The king requested that Becket take his place. He would soon regret this decision.

Task: Examination style response

Read again the source provided earlier in this topic by William FitzStephen.

Write a response to each of the following questions;

a) Why is this source valuable to the historian for an enquiry into the organisation and function of official embassies sent by Henry II?

Explain your answer using the source, the information given about it and your own knowledge of the historical context.

b) How much weight do you give to the evidence of this source for an enquiry into the career of Thomas Becket?

Explain your answer using the source, the information given about it and your own knowledge of the historical context.

Spend no more than 45 minutes on this task

Thomas Becket: A timeline

1118- birth of Thomas Becket

1140s – Becket educated for two years in Paris

1156 – Becket appointed Chancellor

1158 – Becket heads an embassy to King Louis VII

1159 – Becket commands a division of the army besieging Toulouse

1161 – Appointed Archbishop of Canterbury

1164 –Constitution of Clarendon, goes into Exile

1166 – Preaches at Vezelay

1169 – Conferences at Montmirail and Monmatre

1170 – Henry the Young King crowned by Archbishop of York

1170 – November – Becket returns to England

1171 – 25th December – Becket issues a number of excommunications.

1171 – 29th December – Becket murdered

Becket the Archbishop

One major problem with Henry II's aim to have Becket appointed as the new Archbishop of Canterbury was that Becket was not a priest. As an Archdeacon Becket had been part of the Church, but he was not an ordained priest. However, in the face of some opposition by members of the clergy, Becket was ordained as a priest on 2nd June 1161 and the very next day was consecrated Archbishop.

In having Becket appointed Archbishop, Henry II hoped that he would have a strong pillar of support in the Church. Someone who could help him carry through what he saw was much needed reformation of the rights of members of the Church; rights that Henry thought stood in direct challenge to both his kingly authority and to his reforms of secular taxation and law. He was however, mistaken.

Becket seems to have undergone a personality change when he became Archbishop. Formerly extravagant in public, Becket now became ascetic; humble in dress, frugal in diet. He wore hairshirts and coarse robes. He ate sparingly surviving on a diet of water and herbs. Becket now adopted a public demeanour of Christian piety and sternness.

Perhaps one explanation for Becket's transformation was due to the attitude of his fellow churchmen. Despite being an Archdeacon, Becket was seen as primarily a political appointee that had been forced upon them as the head of Church in England. Becket resigned from the post of Chancellor stating that he was unable to fulfil the role of either Archbishop or Chancellor adequately. He could not resign one but he would the other.

Becket's response to this was to prove to everyone that he would fulfil the role of Archbishop of Canterbury to the full extent of his power and authority. In this way Becket was mirroring Henry II himself. Henry II was determined to exert his royal authority to the full; Becket, who had helped and advised and supported Henry II in this endeavour, now determined to do likewise.

As Archbishop, Becket began to exercise his rights straightaway. Manors and castles that had previously been granted to the Church were seized by Becket. He took over possession of Rochester Castle from Henry II; he seized the town of Tunbridge from the Earl of Clare claiming ecclesiastical rights. As Chancellor, a position he still retained, Becket had access to documents that proved the ancestral ownership of these properties.

Becket appointed a priest to oversee a Church in the lands of a Norman baron named William de Eynesford; in doing so Becket overturned an established right that barons formerly held to appoint local priests. When William de Eynesford protested; Becket excommunicated him.

Henry II viewed these events with increasing concern. The seizure of Rochester castle was bad enough, but Henry II had issued a law early in his reign stating that no baron can be excommunicated without his permission. Becket, who as Chancellor, had helped to issue this law was aware that this law had been written on shaky ground and felt confident that he could ignore it. Becket also challenged the payment of Sheriff's Aid in 1163 stating *"it does not become your excellence to deflect something that belongs to another to your use"*.

A confrontation between Henry II and Becket was fast approaching.

Key terms:

Excommunication

An institutional act of religious censure; used to deprive, suspend or limit membership of Church membership. It was a powerful weapon used by the Church on secular lords.

The effect of excommunication was to undermine the authority of the target and in practice if issued against a lord or king for example, the subjects of this individual would be encouraged to not recognise their authority.

Henry's view; the need for Ecclesiastical reform

In 12th century England the Church was a very powerful institution; Henry II would regard the Church as too powerful and a block to his kingly authority. Henry II was not eager to rule as Church leader, but he did want to clearly define the boundaries of Church rights as so far as they might overstep into his own secular authority.

There were apparent concerns for Henry II on a practical level. Anyone who was considered to be a member of the clergy was able to appeal to a church court of law should they fall under suspicion of committing a crime. Before 1160, there had been at least 100 murders in England that might have been committed by Churchmen. These men, these murderers were untouchable by Henry II in a legal sense.

Potentially too, the number of people that could appeal to Church courts rather than be tried in secular law courts was huge; some 15% of Englishmen in the 12th century were technically Churchmen; mostly deacons or church servants. If these men committed crimes they would be tried in Church courts were the punishments were more lenient (Church courts could not torture, mutilate or execute) than in secular courts and fines (*amercements*) would go into Church coffers.

Henry II wanted to simplify matters. Any Churchman who committed a crime should be tried in a secular court of law like anyone else.

The custom of appealing to Rome had also accelerated. This was a trend which had begun under Henry I and became more frequent. On the continent the Emperor Frederick Barbarossa had been excommunicated in 1160 for overstepping his authority over the appointment of bishops. His response had been to encourage an anti-pope in Rome, who had forced the real pope Alexander III into exile. Henry II had no desire to be excommunicated. He therefore wanted to make steps that this could not happen to him through an appeal by a Churchman direct to the Pope.

In 1164 Henry II issued the 'Constitutions of Clarendon'. ***You can read a version of these articles in Appendix 1, Document 1.***

What were the Constitutions of Clarendon?

The Constitutions of Clarendon were a list of articles that were laid before Thomas Becket in March 1164. It was Thomas Becket's refusal to sign these articles that finally forced Becket into exile. The Constitutions comprised 16 points or articles that would guide future law making and recognition of rights.

Henry caused the constitutions of Clarendon to be drawn up by his justiciars primarily in order to pressure Becket to recognise the authority of the king was superior to that of the Church in England. Becket's refusal to agree to these articles was based upon the grounds that they would primarily target and impinge on the rights of the Church.

Henry II was angered by Beckett and applied alternative pressure on him by confiscating the castles of the Eye and Berkhamstead. This pressure seemed to have some effect. Becket seemed to relent and a new council was held a few months later at Northampton.

Northampton and exile

At a new meeting of the Greater Curia a few months later in October 1164, Becket was summoned to appear and this time the openly accused of rejecting the King's authority. Becket was accused of crimes relating to his post of Chancellor. He was accused of embezzling 44000 marks.

Becket retired from the council claiming illness for several days. Then he reappeared in style. In full regalia Becket performed a Mass for the assembled Council and then received hostile challenges to himself and his position. The Earl of Leicester accused him of witchcraft and the Bishop of Exeter renounced his authority; recommending that an embassy be sent to the Pope in order to authorise his replacement. Becket received these accusations calmly and as he began to leave turned and replied that if he had not been a churchman, he would answer his critics with a trial by combat.

Becket then left Northampton and accompanied by only two monks crossed Lincolnshire to reach a ship. From there in November 1164 he went into exile in St Omer in France.

Why were the Constitutions of Clarendon a turning point in the relations between Henry II and Becket?

The articles contained nothing new; there was no new law or right that did not belong by precedent to the crown within them. Becket's refusal to agree to the articles left him with little choice but exile. He did not resign his position and Henry II could not remove him from his post as Archbishop. He could have removed him as Chancellor, but instead did not; others performed the duties of Chancellor, but without the title.

Task: Thomas Becket

What sort of person do you think Thomas Becket was like?

Having read the pen portraits provided above, If you had to use 5 words to describe Thomas Becket – what 5 words would you use?

Exile and opposition

In exile Becket's voice became louder and his position more entrenched. He would remain an exile in France from late 1164 until his return to England in November 1170; shortly before his death.

For almost six years Becket remained out of sight of Henry II, but remained a vocal critic and a thorn in his side. Becket appealed to both Pope Alexander III and King Louis VII.

Louis VII received Becket warmly and housed him in a succession of monasteries and palaces. Becket had been Chancellor of Henry II and therefore knew much about his finances and his policies and concerns. For Louis VII, Becket was a potential gold mine of useful information. Louis VII also knew that by giving Becket a place of refuge he would annoy Henry II and possibly this would give him an advantage the next time they came to blows.

As Archbishop of Canterbury, Becket remained one of the most senior Churchmen in Europe. As such he was in good company. Pope Alexander III himself had been driven out of Rome by the anti-pope Victor. The reason for his exile had been that he had dared to excommunicate the German Emperor Frederick Barbarossa in 1160. Alexander then could well sympathise with Becket. The appeal by the Bishop of Exeter to have him removed failed.

Henry II was clearly aggrieved by Becket. He forced his family and several of his friends to share the exile of Becket; seizing their property as he did.

Becket spent much of his time engaged in correspondence. He wrote many letters to the Pope and also to English Churchmen. The English bishops and barons had largely sided with Henry II in 1164, but the poor and humble people of England seem to have viewed Becket favourably and desired his recall.

In 1166 Becket travelled to Vezelay in France and before a large and receptive audience issued sentences of excommunication upon all who had signed the Constitution of Clarendon. Specifically Becket excommunicated;

- Richard de Luci
- Ranulph de Broc
- Joscelyn of Balliol

This in effect included nearly all the bishops and earls of England. He also excommunicated anyone who had occupied the property of the Archbishop of Canterbury.

The Pope supported Becket; to a point. He was reluctant to see Henry II excommunicated primarily as he saw in Henry a potential ally against Frederick Barbarossa. Henry II was at Chinon when he heard news of Becket's actions at Vezelay and he immediately wrote to the Pope asking for these excommunications to be annulled.

Henry II saw in Becket's actions the hand of King Louis VII. This was an attempt to destabilise his kingship. Henry II responded by threatening to confiscate Church property in England of those religious orders that were harbouring Becket, including the Cistercians. Pope Alexander III agreed with Henry II and ordered religious houses in France not to harbour Becket. Becket therefore had no choice but to seek the hospitality of the French king.

Reconciliation?

Throughout 1166-1169 Henry II and Louis VII were engaged in a series of wars. We shall consider this in more detail elsewhere, but at Montmirail a peace conference between the two kings was arranged in 1169 and it was at Montmirail that Henry II came face to face with Becket for the first time in years. Becket agreed to obey the King; but only insofar as this obedience did not compromise the position of the Church. Henry II again declared that this was an affront to his royal authority. It was almost as it no progress had been made.

However on the 22nd July 1170 the pair met face to face again and were eventually reconciled. Henry II promised to restore the property and privileges he had seized from Becket.

All was well, or so it seemed. Becket made plans to return to England and take up his post of Archbishop once more. But he was reluctant to confront the barons he had excommunicated and driven to fury when he heard the news that in July 1170, Henry's son and heir; also named Henry, had been crowned as *'Rex designatus'* by the Archbishop of York and in the presence of numerous other bishops at Westminster Abbey. This was a clear affront to the Archbishop of Canterbury. Traditionally, only the Archbishop of Canterbury was able to perform a coronation service.

The murder of Becket December 1170

Becket landed in England on the 1st December 1170. He would be dead by the 29th. King Henry II, still on the continent, had provided Becket with a ship but was refused permission to seek out an audience with the newly crowned Henry, the young king. On his arrival Becket was threatened with violence by three barons on the road to Canterbury. The poor that he encountered were overjoyed and celebrated his return.

On Christmas Day 1170 Becket preached the Mass at Canterbury Cathedral and then declared the excommunication of the three barons who had threatened him on the road. On hearing of this sentence the barons immediately took ship and journeyed to the court of Henry II, now on the coast opposite England. These barons told Henry II of the excommunication. For Henry this was news that Becket had not changed his ways. In some frustration, Henry II declared that Becket was;

"...a man who has eaten my bread – a beggar who first came to my court riding a lame pack-horse, with his baggage at his back – shall he insult the king, the royal family, and the whole kingdom, and not

one of these cowards who eat at my table will deliver me from such a turbulent priest?"

Four knights overheard the king – Richard Brito, Hugh de Morville, William Tracey and Reginald Fitzurse. These knights proceeded without delay to cross over to England and on the 29th December 1170 confronted Becket in the Cathedral and there slaughtered him.

Becket's last words were preserved by witnesses. According to these witnesses becket's thoughts at the end were commanding, but concerned for others;

"I resign myself to death; but I forbid you, in the name of the Almighty God, to injure any of those round me, whether monk or layman, great or small."

Reaction to the murder

Europe was hit by the news as by a tremendous shock. Archbishops were not people to be treated so.

The knights seemed to have acted without orders. Henry II on hearing the news of the murder wrote to the Pope and claimed that he was innocent of any complicity in the murder. He would soon undertake an expedition to the furthest part of Europe that he possibly could. He travelled to Ireland to escape the public censure as much as possible.

Others were more welcoming of the news. Becket had angered the barons by his frequent threats and acts of excommunication. They were happy to see him gone. The Archbishop of York declared Becket's death a judgement of heaven.

Others were less pleased. Pope Alexander III threatened to place the whole of England under Interdict as punishment for Becket's murder. King Louis VII of France tried to take advantage of the event. He declared Henry II as complicit in the murder of the Archbishop and urged the Pope to excommunicate Henry II. The people of England had always looked favourably on Becket as a man and priest who would protect them from the taxes and exactions of the King. They began to venerate Becket who was soon afterwards declared a saint. Canterbury became a place of pilgrimage and remains so today.

Avranches 1172

Public sympathy turned against Henry and he was obliged to expressly permit appeals to Rome. Papal influence was to increase in England until it reached its zenith under Innocent III.

At a meeting at Avranches in 1172, Henry II met several Papal legates and was forced to swear that he had taken no part in the murder of Becket and that he had not desired or authorised his death. This helped. But it was not until Henry II conducted his own pilgrimage to Canterbury a few years later in order to publically undergo acts of penance that he was able to begin to overcome the damage done to his prestige.

Task:: The exile of Thomas Becket:

Extract from: From a command issued by Henry II to his sheriffs on 24 December 1164 after Thomas Becket had fled into exile.

"I hereby command you that, if any one, either clerk or lay person, in your bailiwick appeals to the court of Rome, then you are to have him arrested and put under guard until my pleasure shall be known. Also that you seize into your own hands all the revenues and possessions of the archbishop of Canterbury, as Ranulf de Broc** and my other officers shall instruct you.*

*Also I command you to arrest the fathers and mothers, brothers and sisters, nephew and nieces of all the clerks who are with the archbishop, and put them and their chattels*** into my keeping, until my pleasure shall be known, and that you bring this document with you when you are summoned."*

* bailiwick – the area under the authority of a bailiff
** Ranulf de Broc was one of Henry II's supporters. He was granted some of the lands of Canterbury during Becket's exile.
*** chattels – belongings

Why is Source 3 valuable to the historian for an enquiry into Henry II's reaction to Becket's decision to go into exile in 1164?

Explain your answer using the source, the information given about it and your own knowledge of the historical context.

Complete this activity in no more than 20 minutes

2.5 Henry II: Authority and challenges in the years 1161-1172

In this section we will;

- *Explore the main events of Henry II's reign between the years 1161-1172*
- *Continue to explore the medieval source material that deals with Henry II*
- *Consider what England was like during Henry II's reign*
- *Continue to consider the methods by which Henry II would rule*
- *Consider further the relationship between Henry II and Louis VII*
- *Explore the successes and failures of Henry II in the years 1161-72*

Introduction

Henry II had been King of England for several years in 1161. He had established himself as one of the most powerful rulers of Europe in the 12th century and he had done much to restore prosperity to the Kingdom of England. In this section we shall explore the challenges Henry II faced in effectively rule his vast domains?

Henry II reign 1161-1172: a timeline

1161-2 Henry II in Normandy

1164 –Constitution of Clarendon, Becket exiled

1165 – War in Wales

1166 – Rebellion in Brittany

1167 – Rebellion in Aquitaine

1168 – Brittany overrun by Henry II

1169 – Conferences at Montmirail and Monmatre

1170 – Henry the Young King crowned by Archbishop of York

1171 – 29th December – Becket murdered

1171-2 Henry II in Ireland

1172 – Compromise of Avranches

War in Wales 1164-1165

In 1164 the Welsh princes and kings had been at peace with Henry II for some six years. In part the peace had been brought about by Henry's shows of military strength, but also through the retention of hostages. Some Welsh served Henry II as mercenaries in his armies. Others had begun to work for the Anglo-Norman lords that lived on the border between England and Wales.

In 1164 a nephew of the King of South Wales; Rees-ap-Gryffith was found dead under suspicious circumstances. Perhaps he died through natural causes or accident, but Rees-ap-Gryffith understood the death to be murder. He lost no time in gathering his men and supporters and within weeks the Welsh were raiding across the border. The Anglo-Norman barons were unable to adequately prevent these raids; they called for help from Henry II.

In 1165 Henry II invaded Wales with a large army. At first the Welsh appeared to retreat. They seemed reluctant to face such a large army of several thousand men in open combat. Instead the Welsh were awaiting an opportune moment to attack.

They received such an opportunity at Corwen. A severe storm hit Henry's army and disrupted their camps and movements. Taking advantage of the storm the Welsh attacked. The result was a severe defeat for Henry. His army was routed and forced to retreat.

Angered, Henry II ordered the mutilation of his Welsh hostages and prisoners of war. The men had their eyes gouged out, the women suffered the amputation of their ears and noses. All were sent back to Wales as a demonstration of what would happen if the war continued.

The message had its effect and the Welsh lords ended their raids, but the reputation of Henry II was scarcely improved by the episode.

Brittany 1165-1166

Henry had little time to dwell on the affairs in Wales. He was soon required elsewhere, this time in Brittany. Brittany had been governed in Henry's name by Duke Conan IV of Brittany since 1158, but Conan had proved to be an unpopular ruler. He seems to have oppressed and taxed the Bretons heavily and when the Bretons appealed to Henry himself to intervene he had not given satisfaction. Their only remaining option was to rebel.

Conan IV in turn had difficulty in dealing with the rebellion and called upon Henry II to help. Henry transported an army over from England and along with forces from Normandy began to quell the rebellion.

Once Henry was in Brittany, the Bretons now had the opportunity to appeal to him face to face. A delegation of priests voiced the general dissatisfaction with Conan and Henry saw in this an opportunity to make changes that might suit him better.

Conan was forced to resign the Duchy and since he was the earl of Richmond in North Yorkshire, retired to his estates in England. He would be replaced by Conan's heir who was Geoffrey, Henry II's young son who had married Conan's daughter in 1158. Geoffrey was still a minor so in the meantime, Henry would rule Brittany directly in his place.

This arrangement did not suit everyone however. Elements among the Bretons still resented the idea of any outsider ruling them; the Bretons had their own language and customs and in some respects shared more in common with the Welsh and Irish than they did their Norman and French neighbours. As a result much of 1166 was spent by Henry in Brittany stamping out the last embers of rebellion. The rest of the time he was in Normandy and Anjou dealing with a series of rebellions and border incidents in these lands.

Rebellion in Aquitaine 1167-1169

King Louis VII was very interested in the Duchy of Aquitaine. This huge duchy was a land he himself had ruled (through his marriage to Eleanor of Aquitaine) until 1152. That same year, Henry had in turn married Eleanor and now he ruled the Duchy through this same marriage arrangement. Louis VII however retained a keen interest in the affairs of Aquitaine and sought any opportunity he could to exert his influence of the Duchy.

In the 1160s, Louis reacted favourably to the news that two Counts of Aquitaine; those of Angouleme and La Marche were in rebellion. Aquitaine had always been loosely governed by the Dukes of Aquitaine and with Eleanor of Aquitaine effectively confined to England or the presence of Henry II; the Duchy had lacked an effective figurehead to govern. Henry II was not from Aquitaine and could not often visit the Duchy; required as he was in England and Normandy. Again, like Brittany, Aquitaine was culturally and linguistically different from England, Anjou and Normandy. Many lords of the Duchy still looked to the French king for authority or as an alternative to the Angevin Henry.

Henry II had just managed to settle things down in Brittany when he heard news that several major lords in Aquitaine were in rebellion. The main rebels were the Counts of La Marche and Angouleme but they were also joined the Lusignan lords of Poitiers; a minor family that had ambitions. In time some of these ambitions would be fulfilled; Guy of Lusignan would become king in Jerusalem; in part because of this rebellion in Aquitaine that encouraged him to seek his fortune elsewhere.

Henry II spent much of 1167-1168 in Aquitaine bringing these rebel lords to heel. In this he needed help Queen Eleanor was summoned from England and emplaced in the Ducal home of Poitiers in an attempt to satisfy the criticism that Aquitaine had been neglected by its rulers. With her came her son Richard and also an army led by Earl Patrick of Salisbury.

Henry and Earl Patrick together subdued the Aquitainians with horseback raids called *Chevauchees* – devastating horse borne raids that targeted the defenceless peasants and villages from which a feudal lord derived most of their income. The Lusignans were forced to surrender their castle and much of their lands.

Henry II left Aquitaine in 1168 in order to deal with other threats elsewhere – likewise encouraged by the French king. But Earl Patrick and Eleanor remained in Aquitaine. Travelling together near Poitiers, Earl Patrick was killed in an ambush set by the Lusignan brothers Guy and Geoffrey. Queen Eleanor escaped to Poitiers and fighting flared up and continued sporadically until June 1169.

The Conference of Montmirail 1169

In January 1169, King Henry II and King Louis VII met at an arranged meeting at the fortress of Montirail, in the County of Maine.

The past few years had been turbulent; Henry II and Louis VII had been engaged in military conflicts; not only with each other, but they had also been encouraging certain tenants in chief of each other to cause localised rebellions and conflict. The result had been the rebellions in Brittany and in Aquitaine.

Part of the reason for these conflicts had come about through concern for the future. Both kings were now middle aged and whilst Henry II had potential heirs aplenty; Louis VII had fathered no male heir until 1165 when Philip Augustus was born to Louis VII's third wife. Both men were concerned that their sons and heirs would have a respectable inheritance. Moreover, both families were heavily inter-connected. Henry II's eldest son and heir Henry (the future Young King) was already married to Margaret, the daughter of Louis VII.

What would happen if the young Henry decided to contest the claim of Philip Augustus? Would all France be ruled by the Angevins? This was a great concern for Louis VII; as a result he had pursued a policy of encouraging disorder for his great rival Henry II. The rebellions in Aquitaine were encouraged by Louis VII; another way in which Louis had tried to unbalance Henry II was through his sheltering of Thomas Becket.

If things continued there was every chance that Henry II would experience some disaster. Henry II could not be everywhere and sooner or later he would have too much trouble to deal with.

In some ways the advantage was with the French King. His eastern frontier was stable and secure. It was only those lands facing Henry II that were regularly threatened. Louis VII had fewer lands, but he could reach threatened regions much quickly and with greater concentration of his own resources. He did not need to worry about lands separated by seas that were culturally and linguistically different.

The Conference of Montmirail then was a good opportunity for both rulers to meet and assure each other that they had no designs on each other's territory.

At Montmirail in 1169 Henry II declared to Louis VII that his sons would share the inheritance that he would bequeath on them. Henry II would not attempt to keep his Angevin Empire whole under the sole control of his heir; instead he would divide his lands as follows;

- Henry – the Kingdom of England, the Duchy of Normandy and the County of Anjou.
- Richard – the Duchy of Aquitaine.
- Geoffrey – the Duchy of Brittany.
- John – no land as yet allocated.

This was not all. Henry's sons were required to give homage to Louis VII for all of their continental lands. In this way the French king would be overlord of both Richard and Geoffrey for their Duchies and Henry would give homage for both Normandy and Anjou. In effect this would mean that the clock would be rewound to 1152.

Louis VII confirmed this division and moreover it was agreed that Richard would marry Louis' daughter Alice. This agreement resulted in peace between Henry and Louis.

Task: The Conference of Montmirail

The conference of Montmirail in 1169 was intended to result in peace between Henry and Louis, to secure the future roles of Henry's sons and an end to rebellions.

What potential problems can you identify from the following factors;

- *The division of territory amongst Henry's sons.*
- *The lack of land for John*
- *The arranged marriages of French princesses with Henry and Richard*
- *A return to the territorial divisions of 1152*
- *Requirement to give homage to the French King for their lands*

Write a sentence or two for each of the above bullets

Henry under pressure 1170-1171

In 1170-1171 Henry II was widely criticised throughout Europe because of the murder of Becket. Henry was a king who had the blood of an Archbishop on his hands, whether he had ordered it or not, was under diplomatic pressure.

The commons of England had always seen Becket as a man who looked to protect them against the barons and earls of England. In death Becket was even more popular. King Louis VII openly referred to Henry II as a murderer, even Pope Alexander III, who had been broadly supportive of Henry II was now wavering. Henry might be excommunicated, England placed under Interdict. Despite his repeated statements of denial of any complicity in; Henry II was on the defensive.

One way in which Henry II could act was to remove himself from the situation, but he needed to be visible to his subjects and tenants in chief in order to exert his authority. In late 1171 Henry II saw that several of these tenants in chief had been acting rather too independently. He would pay them a visit, in Ireland.

Ireland in the 12th century

In the 12th century Ireland was a Christian land, ruled by numerous kings. These kings ruled kingdoms such as Ulster, Connaught, Leinster, Meath and Munster. The High King of Ireland was a position of first amongst equals – appointed at Tara; a sacred hill which still emanated the pagan traditions of Ireland.

Ireland had its own customs and institutions and the Irish spoke *Gaelic* – a language very distinct to the French spoken by Henry II and the Anglo-Norman barons. The Irish Christian Church too was distinct and rich in monasteries, perhaps due to its proximity to pagan customs and institutions which were still in existence. Great manuscripts were produced in Ireland including the *Book of Kells* – which remains one of the greatest examples of monastic illumination in existence.

Ireland was on the edge of Europe, it had largely remained apart and sheltered from the events that had affected Europe in the past few centuries, and most rulers of Europe had paid little attention to what happened in Ireland. However Ireland, like England had seen attacks by Scandinavian raiders – the Vikings in the 8th-10th centuries, and like England, parts of Ireland had subsequently been settled by these same Scandinavians – with settlers from Denmark and Norway establishing settlements such as at Dublin.

However, Ireland was increasingly coming to the attention of the rest of Europe. Trade and communication between Ireland and the rest of the British Isles was well established and lords on both sides of the Irish Sea had been in communication for centuries. It was only natural then that should there be any turmoil in Ireland or England, Scotland or Wales; appeals for assistance could be sent across the Irish Sea.

Ireland and the Anglo-Norman invasion 1169-1170

The Popes of Rome were increasingly interested in ensuring that the Irish Church take the party line of mainstream Catholicism. In 1155, Henry II had received permission from the Pope, Adrian IV (the only Englishman ever to be Pope) to invade Ireland if he so desired. Henry II had declined at the time; he had his hands full in settling England after the Anarchy and controlling his vast continental possessions.

In 1168 the Irish King of Leinster Diarmait MacMurchada was involved in a war with a local rival. In the course of one raid he kidnapped the wife of Tiernan O'Rourke; a rival ruler.

This local war escalated. The Irish High King Ruaidri ua Conchobair arranged a coalition against Diarmait MacMurchada and forced him into exile.

Diarmait MacMurchada crossed the Irish Sea and reaching the European mainland, appealed for help from Henry II. Henry II was busy with Aquitaine and with Louis VII at the time, but with Henry's permission Diarmait MacMurchada was permitted to seek the assistance of the Anglo-Norman Barons of England and Wales in reinstating him to Leinster.

Several barons answered Diarmait MacMurchada's call; Maurice FtzGerald, Robert FitzStephen and primarily Richard de Clare, Earl of Pembroke and nicknamed 'Strongbow'.

Diarmait MacMurchada arranged a marriage between his daughter Eva and Strongbow and whilst Strongbow recruited a larger army, Robert FitzStephen crossed over to Leinster with Diarmait MacMurchada.

FitzStephen landed in Ireland in 1169 with a small army of about 500 men. Many of these men however were landless knights. With Diarmait MacMurchada's own forces, together they captured the town of Wexford. In response the Irish High King's coalition declared Diarmait MacMurchada a national enemy.

Strongbow arrived in Ireland in early 1170 with an army of 2000-2500 men – again with a high proportion of landless knights. Strongbow and FitzStephen combined their forces and captured the town of Waterford before marching on Dublin, which rapidly surrendered. The barons had conquered large swathes of land in Ireland in a short amount of time. Diarmait MacMurchada died in early 1171 and Strongbow was married to his daughter; he now had claim to become King of Leinster.

Henry and Ireland 1171-2

Henry II was kept informed of events in Ireland throughout 1170 and increasingly he saw that young landless knights saw in Ireland an opportunity to carve out their own lands and territories in a land that was not under the authority of himself. Great lords such as Strongbow and FitzStephen would soon be in possession of large amounts of lands – that they owned themselves with no authority over them.

For Henry II this was intolerable. He did not desire his tenants-in-chief setting up their own independent lands. He ordered that no subject of his should go to Ireland. Those in Ireland were recalled and to leave Ireland before Easter 1171 under threat of forfeiting their estates and titles and suffering exile. Before this deadline passed, Henry II ordered that Strongbow's estates confiscated. This heavy application of pressure was not intended to punish Strongbow- rather it was pressure designed to force Strongbow and his companions to acknowledge that Henry II was their lord and king.

Strongbow however was preoccupied with his own troubles. A confederation of Irish and Danish forces attacked Strongbow at Dublin in 1171. Strongbow was forced onto the defensive. The stream of reinforcements he had been receiving from England and Wales was stopped by Henry's orders. In desperation Strongbow appealed in person for help from Henry II.

Henry II agreed to help. Strongbow would surrender his Irish conquests to Henry, in return he would have his lands and titles in England and Wales restored.

Henry II sailed to Ireland in October 1171 from Milford in South Wales. He had with him an army of some 5-6000 men. He landed at Waterford on the 18th October 1171 and received the homage of the Anglo-Norman barons present in Ireland. From Waterford, Henry II marched on Dublin and there was crowned king of Ireland in the presence of several Irish rulers as well as his assembled tenants in chief. The Kings of Ulster and Connaught however rejected Henry II and the Island of Ireland became divided between the native rulers in the North and along the Atlantic coast, and the new Anglo-Norman ruled kingdom of Ireland in the South and East.

Henry II resided in Ireland until April 1172 and spent this time confirming his Anglo-Norman tenants in possession of their lands and titles. In this he was assisted by the majority of the Irish Church and Pope Alexander III ratified Henry II's arrangements in Ireland.

In the Anglo-Norman tradition these lords built for themselves a series of castles from which to rule – no less than 23 were constructed within a few years in County Louth alone and several great examples of castle building from the 12th century remain today – including Trim Castle – built by Justiciar Hugh de Lacy and his son Walter.

Peace did not come to Ireland after Henry II's visit. War continued sporadically between the Anglo Normans and the Irish throughout 1172-1175, but a peace was reached in 1175 at the Treaty of Windsor in 1175 between Henry II and high King Ruaidri that agreed a division of the island and by 1177 Henry had appointed a Justiciar for Ireland; Hugh de Lacy.

Trim Castle in Ireland

Task: Examination style response

Below is a question taken from the Edexcel Exam AS History Paper set in 2016

From Gerald of Wales, The Conquest of Ireland, written in 1189. Gerald was archdeacon of Brecon and a chronicler. In 1184 he became a chaplain and royal clerk in Henry II's court. He travelled extensively in Wales and Ireland and accompanied Henry II on an expedition to Ireland in 1185.

"The valiant King Henry landed in Ireland in the seventeenth year of his reign, being the year of our Lord 1172. While Henry was resting a few days at Wexford, the men of Wexford, to court his favour, brought to him their prisoner Fitz-Stephen, who was bound in chains. These men tried excusing themselves because it was Fitz-Stephen who had been the first to invade Ireland without the royal licence, and he had set the others a bad example. The King, having loudly rebuked Fitz-Stephen, and threatened him with his anger for his foolish enterprise, at last sent him back, bound and chained, to be kept in safe custody in Reginald's Tower**. Soon afterwards, Dermitius, king of Cork, came of his own free will and made his submission to the King of England, doing homage and swearing fealty to the English king as his lord, and giving hostages for the regular payment of a yearly homage. The King of England thence marched to Cashel. There Duvenald, king of Limerick, came to meet him and having asked for peace, which was granted, became also a subject of the King and did him fealty which he promised faithfully to observe. Indeed there was scarcely anyone of name or rank who did not pay to the King the homage due from a liegeman to his lord.*

** Fitz-Stephen was Gerald of Wales' uncle*

*** Reginald's Tower – a defensive tower which was used as a prison*

How much weight do you give to the evidence this passage for an enquiry into Henry II's extension of control in Ireland in 1172?

Explain your answer using the source, the information given about it and your own knowledge of the historical context.

Complete your response in no more than 30 minutes

Task: Extended response

Write a response to the following question;

"The extension of Angevin territories in the years 1154-72 was achieved mainly by Henry II's military skill"

To what extent does the evidence support this view?

Complete your response in no more the 45 minutes

PART THREE: Rule and reform

Part Three: Rule and reform

3.1 The King and his Court

3.2 The Justiciars and the Exchequer

3.3 Regulating the power of the Nobility: The Knights, Barons and Earls

3.4 Law and order in 12th century England

3.5 The State of England under Henry II

3.1 The King and his court

In this section we will;

- *Continue to explore the medieval source material that deals with Henry II*
- *Consider the extent of the need of Henry to have a travelling court*
- *Understand what the Curia Regis was and begin to understand how it operated*
- *Understand what Justiciars were and what they did*
- *Understand what the Exchequer was and what it did*
- *Consider the extent to which each major office of state needed to work in unison*

Introduction

When Henry became King of England in 1154 he had a problem greater than any of his predecessors on the English throne. How could he effectively rule his vast domains?

Henry and communication across his lands

King Henry II was an energetic and active ruler for almost the entirety of his reign. He had to be. The Kingdom of England, the Duchies of Normandy, Aquitaine and the Counties of Anjou, Maine, and Touraine would also be supplemented in time by additional territories in Wales and Ireland.

Each region required regular visits by the king in person if he were to guarantee that his instructions and laws were being carried out. Today, we can travel by airplane, car and train as well as ships. These journeys now are fast, relatively cheap and above all safe. We travel on established networks of roads and services between towns and cities are generally regular.

King Henry II had none of these advantages.

Sailing across the English Channel between England and Normandy was often a dangerous undertaking. The risk of shipwreck or drowning was a very real one. If the winds were strong or blowing in the wrong direction a ship might not be able to leave port for days or even weeks.

On land the situation was hardly better. Road networks were often poor or even non-existent. At best Henry could use in places the remains of the old Roman road networks which had been constructed hundreds of years earlier. More typically Henry would travel along track ways – created by local farmers to move their livestock or wagons and often impassable when transformed to mud in poor weather.

On the move

For King Henry II, to establish a single capital as a place from which to rule would result in neglecting all the other regions not within easy proximity to this location. The only alternative to this would be to adopt a nomadic lifestyle; not just for himself but for the entire court.

So, if King Henry decided to establish a permanent capital in London for example, it would be almost impossible to effectively govern Aquitaine as the distance was too large.

On traveling with the King;

Peter of Blois was a secretary to King Henry II. He has left an intriguing description of life on the road with King Henry II;

"If the king has promised to remain in a place for a day – and particularly if he has announced his intention publicly by the mouth of a herald – he is sure to upset all the arrangements by departing early in the morning. As a result you see men dashing around as if they were mad, beating their packhorses, running their carts into one another – in short giving a lively imitation of Hell. If, on the other hand, the king orders an early start, he is certain to change his mind, and you can take it for granted that he will sleep until midday. Then you will see the packhorses loaded and waiting, the courtiers dozing, traders fretting, and everyone grumbling. People go to ask the maids and the doorkeepers what the king's plans are, for they are the only people likely to know the secrets of the court. Many a time when the king was sleeping a message would be passed from his chamber about the city or town he planned to go to, and although there was nothing certain about it, it would rouse us all up. After hanging about aimlessly for so long we would be comforted by the prospect of good lodgings. This would produce such a clatter of horse and foot that all Hell seemed let loose. But when our courtiers had gone ahead almost the whole day's ride, the king would turn aside to some other place where he had, it might be, just a single house with accommodation for himself and no one else. I hardly dare say it, but I believe that in truth he took a delight in seeing what a fix he puts us in. after wandering some three or four miles in an unknown wood, and often in the dark, we thought ourselves lucky if we stumbled upon some filthy little hovel. There was often a sharp and bitter argument about a mere hut, and swords were drawn for possession of lodgings that pigs would have shunned".

Peter of Blois; serving as a secretary to Henry II

The 'Curia Regis' (The King's Court)

The King's Court - The Curia Regis - was the heart of King Henry II's government.

The Curia Regis could be divided into two interlinked but separate bodies; the Major Curia Regis and the Minor Curia Regis. The Curia Regis was the heart of government for kings of England from 1066 until 1215 and the advent of Magna Carta. As such it was the precursor of Parliament.

The 'Major or irregular Curia Regis' –aka the '*Magnum Concilium*'

The Major Curia Regis was originally known as the Curia Regis and was the assembly of the major nobles and churchmen of the realm. This body still existed but met infrequently and on major occasions, for example over Christmas at an agreed location where the King would meet these elite members of society. The focus of the Major Curia Regis would be on the concerns and issues relating to the major landowners and some matters of discussion on foreign affairs. But it would also be a time of great festivity and celebration. Hunts would be organised and great banquets arranged. It was a good opportunity for the Earls and important barons of England to settle any disputes between themselves and curry favour with the King.

The Curia Regis – the King's court

The main focus of our attention is now directed to the 'Minor Curia Regis'. This Curia Regis was the true heart of the government of King Henry II and unlike the Major Curia Regis, it travelled with the king and met extremely frequently; for this reason we will continue to refer to this body as the Curia Regis.

The Curia Regis was a travelling convoy that comprised of the King, his family (when present), the King's ministers, clerks and secretaries; his counsellors and servants as well as the King's own household knights and attached men at arms.

At any given time the Curia Regis would number several hundred individuals at the very least. One Secretary of Henry II, Walter Map speaks of thousands of people. Because the Curia Regis travelled, its numbers changed as people joined the cortege or left on order of the king.

In spite of the Curia Regis being a travelling organisation. It comprised of several separate institutions; each of which formed an integral part of the King's government. The major components of the Curia Regis were as follows;

- *The Chancellery*
- *The Chamber/ The Wardrobe*
- *The Chapel*
- *The Kitchen*
- *The Transportation*
- *The Household Knights*

We shall explore each of these departments in a little more detail;

The Chancellery

The Chancellery was that part of the Curia Regis which was responsible for creating and issuing documents and decrees that had been issued by the king. When King Henry II pronounced a command or order – this order would be written up by the Clerks and Secretaries of the Chancellery and distributed from this office.

The Chancellery was headed by a minster titled the Chancellor. This role had been formed in England in 1066 with the accession of William the Conqueror to the throne of England.

Often the Chancellor was a priest of clergyman and perhaps the most famous Chancellor from the reign of Henry II was Thomas Beckett.

How do we know about the Curia Regis?

Much of our knowledge of the workings and procedures of the Curia Regis comes from Ranulf de Glanville's important book;

'Tractatus de legibus et consuetudinibus regni Anglie' or in English 'The Treatise on the Laws and Customs of the Kingdom of England'.

Today this work is better known as 'Glanvill'.

The Seal of Henry II

The Chamber/ The Wardrobe

The office of the Chamber was despite its name a very important part of the Curia Regis. The King required money in order to govern his kingdom and pay for everything. It was the Chamber that was the office that was responsible for receiving and the expenditure of money required by the King.

The Minister of the Chamber was the Chamberlain. It was the Chamberlain who was accountable for the King's expenditure whilst on tour. In this he was assisted by Clerks and Secretaries. As you can imagine, the office of Chamberlain was one of the most important positions that there was as the King would want someone he could trust when it came to his money.

The Wardrobe was not just for clothes as you might otherwise expect. It was the office that was responsible for keeping the money carried around with the King as he travelled his lands. Money could also be deposited and stored (or taken from) Royal Castles; strongpoints scattered across the King's lands and providing a secure location for money and wealth of the king to be stored in their treasuries. The Chamberlain also provided money for expenses incurred by all the other parts of the Curia Regis.

The Chapel and Almonry

The King's Curia Regis was accompanied by churchmen. These priests were important as they provided spiritual guidance for the King and provided Church services for him as he travelled. The Almonry also dispensed charity to the poor and needy as the Curia Regis travelled.

The Kitchen

The King and his Curia Regis needed food – a lot of it. This office was as essential as any of the others as it provided food and sustenance for the king and the Curia Regis. Servants would procure food as the Curia Regis travelled or prepare the carcasses of animals killed by his kings and attendants when they hunted.

Transportation

The Curia Regis travelled. Since it travelled it needed wagons, carts and horses and oxen to pull these wagons. The Curia Regis would be most easily identifiable on the road by the sheer number of carts and wagons on the roads. These wagons needed men to drive them, men to repair them (Coopers) and men and boys to groom and feed the animals that pulled these wagons. Perhaps more people worked in this part of the Curia Regis than in any other.

The Household Knights

The Household Knights were another indispensable part of the Curia Regis. More strictly speaking they were part of the King's household (*The familia regis*). The household knights were the King's friends and companions and included his stewards – the men that attended to the person of the King as well as his own servants.

The Household Knights served as the King's bodyguard but were not limited to this important duty. They were also his confidants and advisors and also served as the King's messengers to the Earls and barons and when required, the Household knights could be used by the King as 'a posse' used to capture or arrest those suspected of criminal activity. It has been estimated that King Henry II had at any one time around one hundred knights in attendance at the Curia Regis.

Task: Examination style response

Read again the source provided earlier in this topic - (Peter of Blois *'On travelling with the King')*

Write a response to each of the following questions;

a) Why is this source valuable to the historian for an enquiry into the organisation and function of the Curia Regis?

Explain your answer using the source, the information given about it and your own knowledge of the historical context.

b) How much weight do you give to the evidence of this source for an enquiry into the workings of the Curia Regis?

Explain your answer using the source, the information given about it and your own knowledge of the historical context.

Spend no more than 45 minutes on this task

THE CURIA REGIS

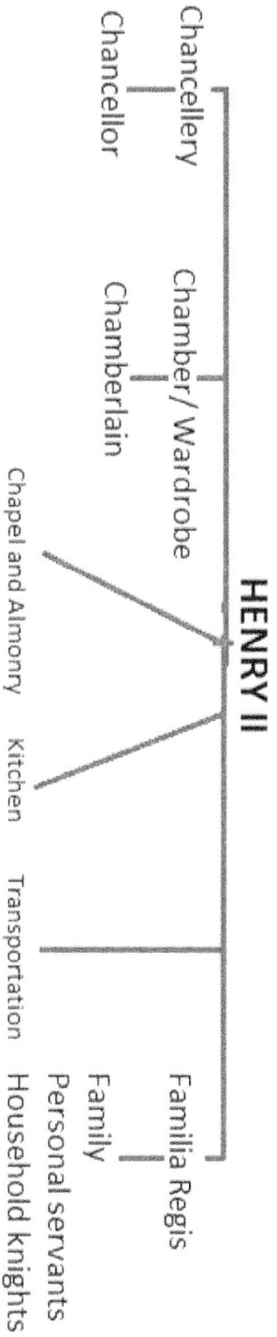
HENRY II
Chancellery
Chancellor
Chamber/ Wardrobe
Chamberlain
Chapel and Almonry
Kitchen
Transportation
Familia Regis
Family
Personal servants
Household knights

3.2 The Justiciars and the Exchequer

In this section we will;

- *Understand what Justiciars were and what they did*
- *Understand what the Exchequer was and what it did*
- *Consider the extent to which each major office of state needed to work in unison*

Introduction

When Henry became King of England in 1154 he had a problem greater than any of his predecessors on the English throne. How could he effectively rule his vast domains?

The importance of delegation

It is clear that the King could not be everywhere at once – despite attempts to move as much as possible around his lands.

If King Henry II was to effectively govern his vast domains he would need to delegate some of his authority to responsible individuals, who could remain in a region and in the absence of the King, be able to act in King Henry II's name.

Not all of the government officials and state administrative offices accompanied the Curia Regis on its travels. We shall now look at two of the major institutions – Justiciars and the Exchequer.

Justiciar

During the reign of King Henry II the most senior government official below the King was the Justiciar; also known as the Chief Justiciar. In the absence of the King, the Justiciar was his representative and the chief political and judicial officer.

The Justiciars had duties that were wide ranging. They would receive ambassadors in the absence of the King, they would summon and preside over courts of law. The Justiciar would deal with day to day business of running and administering the region for which they were responsible. The Justiciar could issue orders under his own seal of writ and also could preside over the exchequer. The Justiciar would even, if necessary lead armies on military campaigns.

In England there was a chief Justiciar who was often assisted by a sub-ordinate or co-Jusiticiar. In the Duchy of Normandy, King Henry II also gave similar powers of authority to an individual with the title of Seneschal. Once King Henry II had occupied parts of Ireland he also appointed a Justiciar for his lands there also.

Three Justiciars of the reign of King Henry II

In England the office of Justiciar was held by three men during the reign of King Henry II;

- Robert de Beaumont 1154-68
- Richard de Luci 1154-1179
- Ranulf de Glanville 1180-1189

As can be seen, each Justiciar held the position for a long period of time. The office of Justiciar was not a fixed term appointment, but a Justiciar could be relieved of his position at any time by the king; as happened to Ranulf de Glanville by Richard I after he became King in 1189.

Robert de Beaumont 1154-68

Robert de Beaumont was the Earl of Leicester and until 1153, Robert was a staunch supporter of King Stephen. Robert had been heavily rewarded by King Stephen and supported him throughout the Anarchy; however by 1153 Robert had evidently decided that he would switch his loyalty to Henry.

One of the main reasons for this was probably due to land. As an Anglo-Norman baron, Robert possessed lands in England and also in Normandy, but during the Anarchy Robert's lands in Normandy were confiscated. In May 1153 Earl Robert formally switched allegiance to Henry and duly had his lands in Normandy restored to him.

On the accession of King Henry II to the throne of England in December 1154, Henry II appointed Robert de Beaumont, Earl of Leicester to the position of Justiciar. He would remain in this post until his death in 1168.

Richard de Luci

Richard de Luci was an English lord that served as both Sheriff of Essex and Hertfordshire, but also served as a subordinate Justiciar alongside Robert de Beaumont. On the death of Robert de Beaumont in 1168, Richard de Luci served as Justiciar in England until he in turn died in 1179.

Ranulf de Glanville

Ranulf de Glanville was Justiciar from 1180 until he was sacked by the newly crowned King Richard I in 1189 – who replaced him with men he could trust more.

Ranulf de Glanville is perhaps the most famous of King Henry II's Justiciars as it was he who wrote the *'Tractatus de legibus et consuetudinibus regni Anglie'* or in English *'The Treatise on the Laws and Customs of the Kingdom of England'*. Today this work is better known as *'Glanvill'.*

Ranulf de Glanville was a Sheriff before he became Justiciar – in Yorkshire, Warwickshire and Leicester between the years 1163-1170. Ranulf was subsequently removed under suspicion of corruption during the Inquest of the Sheriffs in 1170, but was reappointed as Sheriff of Lancashire in 1173, Sheriff of Westmoreland in 1174 and as Sheriff led forces in the Great Rebellion – even capturing King William the Lion at Alnwick in 1174.

In 1175 Ranulf de Glanville became Sheriff of Yorkshire and in 1176 appointed a Justice itinerant of the King's Court and also Custodian of Queen Eleanor after the Great Rebellion. In 1180 Ranulf de Glanville was appointed Justiciar and served in this position until relieved by Richard I. Thereafter it appears that Ranulf joined the Third Crusade and died at the siege of Acre in 1190.

The Treasury of England: The Exchequer

Money, money and yet more money. The King of England needed money in order to be able to effectively run his kingdom. Money was required to pay for the King and his travelling court; the Curia Regis, it was also required for paying for his armies, building his castles and ships and also to help to pay the necessary expenses of diplomacy. Some Historians; including John Gillingham have sometimes described England as effectively a bank- from which kings like Henry II could draw upon in order to exert his power and authority over all of his lands.

There is some strong evidence for seeing England as a single large bank from which the king might draw wealth. Henry II was also keen to see that the fortunes of this bank developed and improved.

In 1154 the income of England, devastated by the civil war of the Anarchy was around £10,500. According to the piep rolls of the time, by the end of King Henry II's reign in 1189, England could provide him with an income of around £22,000.

What was the Exchequer?

The Exchequer as an office was established by the latest in 1110 and was the greatest administrative office of the Kingdom of England. The Exchequer was (and remains) the state treasury of the Country.

The Exchequer takes its name from the chequered cloth that was placed on tables which were used to receive the documents that notified the treasury of money debts that were owed to the king from a variety of sources.

The Exchequer was based initially at Winchester – but at some date in the 12th century the Exchequer was transferred to Westminster and it was housed in rooms within the palace of Westminster in chambers just off the Great Hall built by King William Rufus.

The head of the Exchequer was the Justiciar as mentioned above, however, the day to day running and oversight of the Exchequer was the 'Treasurer of the Exchequer' often shortened just to 'Treasurer'.

What was the function of the Exchequer?

The primary function of the Exchequer was to raise revenue for the King. Each year the Exchequer received notifications of money that would be owed to it in the form of written documents rolled up in scrolls. These were called 'Pipe Rolls' after their shape. These Pipe Rolls remain a very useful historical source of information on the wealth and ability of the country to be able to fund the king and his projects.

The revenue received from the Exchequer would be then spent or saved in a variety of ways;

- It could be forwarded to the King's Wardrobe
- It could be spent directly by the Exchequer on the King's orders
- It could be stored in the Treasury at Westminster
- It could be stored in Royal Castles

We are fortunate that we know quite a lot about the running and organisation of the Exchequer due to the existence of a book; the *'Dialogus de Scaccario'* which was written by a treasurer who served King Henry II; his name was Richard FitzNeal.

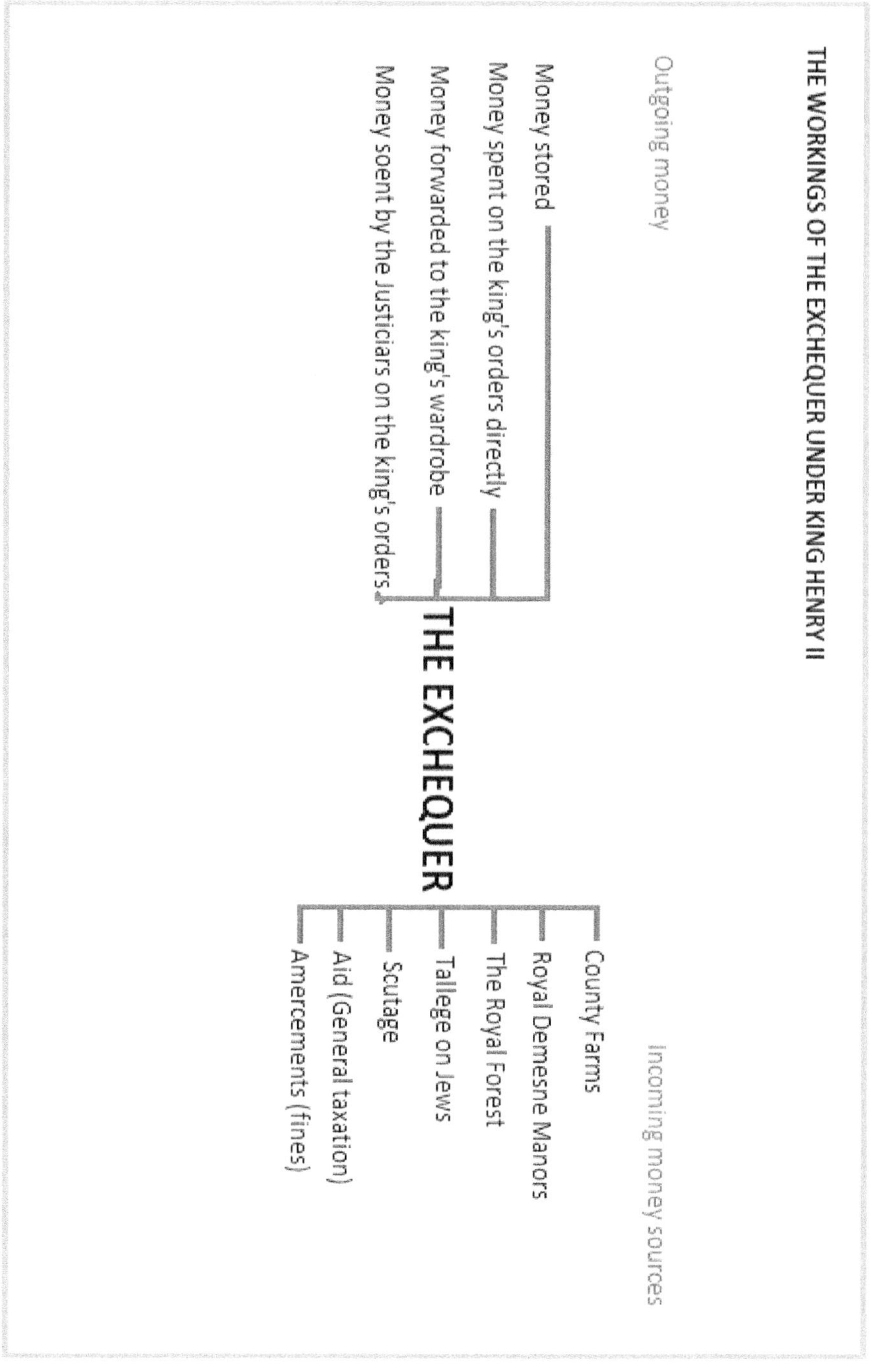
THE WORKINGS OF THE EXCHEQUER UNDER KING HENRY II
Outgoing money
Money stored
Money spent on the king's orders directly
Money forwarded to the king's wardrobe
Money soent by the Justiciars on the king's orders
THE EXCHEQUER
Incoming money sources
County Farms
Royal Demesne Manors
The Royal Forest
Tallege on Jews
Scutage
Aid (General taxation)
Amercements (fines)

Where did the Exchequer get its money from?

The diagram overleaf depicts a simplified way in which the Exchequer both received and spent the money that flowed into and out of it.

We shall now provide a brief explanation of some of the sources of money that the Exchequer could draw upon. This list is not exhaustive and there were other sources;

- County Farms
- Royal Demesne Manors
- The Royal Forest
- Tallege on Jews
- Scutage
- Aid (General taxation)
- Amercements (fines)

County Farms

England was divided for administrative purposes into thirty eight Counties. Each County, from the smallest Rutland, to the largest, Yorkshire, was required to pay into the Exchequer a set amount annually – this was known as the 'Farm'. The set amount known was called the 'County Farm'.

The County Farm was to be paid by the Sheriff. The Sheriff raised this money from fines (*amercements*) from local courts, traditional payments (such as sheriff's aid) and manors owned by the king, but run by the Sheriff.

Royal Demesne Manors

Royal Demesne Manors were farming communities of various sizes that were owned by the King and as such were part of his wealth and sources of his income. These manor farms also paid into the Exchequer.

Scutage

Major and minor landowners that owed scutage were baron, earl or knight that owed knight service to the King in return for the land they occupied. When demanded, each of these landowners were required to send a full quota of knights to serve the King.

Scutage was the name given to money that was owed by a landowner in lieu of sending this quota of knights and in practice was charged annually. The landowner would then reimburse himself for the expense of scutage by re-compensating himself from the knights in question.

Tallege on the Jews

Tallege was a tax that was issued according to the whim or need of the King. There were several kinds of tallege; including on individual towns and cities in England.

Tallege on the Jews was often a nice windfall for King Henry II. The Jewish community in England in the 12th century was often involved in merchant trading and money lending. In particular the Jews of England would lend money to those best able to repay – the Barons and Earls, but sometimes these lords were reluctant or otherwise unable to repay these loans. Should the king impose a tallege on the Jews then, this loan and its' debt could be transferred to the King. This debt would therefore by repayable by the lord to the king directly; further obligating the lord to the King.

The Royal Forest

In the 12th century, large parts (estimated at between a third or a quarter of the total land) of the country of England was defined as the 'Royal Forest'. This Royal Forest was considered by the King to part of his own wealth and income and as a result income drawn from this source was paid direct to the Exchequer. The Royal Forest was a major source of the King's English revenue.

Do not think of the Royal Forest as one, single indivisible woodland with clear borders. Rather it was a huge series of regions, with people and communities dwelling within these areas. Instead, it may be more useful to envisage a modern National Park – such as the Peak District.

Legally, the Royal Forest was not subject to 'Common Law' and income raised from it could be raised arbitrarily by the will of the King. Revenue from the Royal Forest could take the following forms;

Amercements (fines) - from those who poached wild animals from the Royal Forest such as deer, stags and boars.

Purpresture – the construction of buildings within the Royal Forest

Waste – tree felling within the Royal Forest

Assart – land clearance for fields

Aid

Aid was a term used to describe general taxation. Aid was payable by all inhabitants of England and was assessed according to the ability to pay. The richer you were – the more you might pay. It was payable either in coins or goods and your ability to pay was assessed on your land, the yield of your crops and the number of livestock.

A late example of an Aid was the so called Saladin Tithe instituted in 1189 which was to pay towards the military expeditions of the Kings in the Third Crusade. Only those who took the cross as a Crusader were exempt, others were liable to a 10% tax on their property and moveable wealth.

Amercements

Amercements were fines imposed by courts of law. These could be minor fines for minor infringements such as poaching, or could consist of the entire property and wealth of a criminal who had been executed or those declared as outlaws.

Other sources

Other sources of income for the Exchequer (and therefore the King) included the Sheriff's aid and income drawn from the property of orphans and female heirs.

There were also more extraordinary payments paid direct to the King who may or may not transfer these funds back to the Exchequer. Such payments may include 'gifts' from other rulers, or a thankyou from a young man entering upon his inheritance. Likewise, an otherwise landless knight might, on marriage to a female heiress donate some of his new found wealth to the King, who would have facilitated this marriage to the heiress.

Coinage reforms of Henry II

When Henry II became king of England in December 1154, the Exchequer was exhausted through the long period of civil war but it was also exhausted because the coinage of England had become devalued and debased.

During the Anarchy there were numerous lords, all recruiting mercenaries, who worked for silver coinage and plunder. Plunder came from opponents, however the coinage came from the lord.

As a result of the need for lords to acquire coins they established private mints (where coins were made) and produced a variety of coins of differing weight and silver content. There was therefore no single established currency in England.

Steps had been taken by King Stephen and Henry together in 1153 with the closure of several unauthorised mints and the production of standardised silver coinage. The coins of 1153 until 1158 were called ***Awbridge silver pennies***.

Further reform was still required however and in 1158 Henry II reformed the coins again and further reduced the number of producing mints to a dozen or so locations. These mints were in the larger towns of England such as London, York, Lincoln and Exeter. In addition to a consistent set of weights, the 1158 coins also had a further innovation; Henry II had his names inscribed upon them.

Short coin of Henry II

In 1180 the coinage was reformed again with the introduction of the 'Short Cross' silver coins. These coins were now produced at only ten mints in the larger towns across England. The silver content of the 'Short Cross' coins was purer than previous editions and remained in circulation not only throughout the remainder of Henry II's reign; the coins continued in circulation (including with the name 'HENRI') through the reigns of Kings Richard I and King John.

Stabilising the currency helped to increase the prosperity of England as can be seen from information recorded in the Exchequer pipe rolls. In 1154 the amount of money received by the Exchequer was approximately £12,000. In the years 1154-1166 the average income received by the Exchequer was £18,000 and in 1166-1189 the average income received by the Exchequer was £22,000.

Task: King Henry II and the Exchequer

Write a response to the following question;

To what extent do you agree with the view that King Henry II's main sources of income were drawn from his own property?

Spend no more than 30 minutes on this question

3.3 Regulating the power of the Nobility: Knights, Barons and Earls

In this section we will;

- *Understand what Knights, Barons and Earls were and what they did*
- *Understand what Scutage was*
- *Understand what the Cartae Baronum was and its implications*
- *Consider the extent to which each office of state needed to work in unison*

Introduction

When Henry became King of England in 1154 he had a problem greater than any of his predecessors on the English throne. How could he effectively rule his vast domains? One group of people key to Henry II remaining as King were the large landowners; his tenents in chief – the Earls and Barons of England.

Domesday 1086

In 1086 William the Conqueror had ordered that all of the people and lands of England be recorded so that he could determine how much money he could draw upon from his subjects. This record was the Domesday Book and it was a great success. It allowed William and his successors to assess and raise taxes based upon the wealth of England.

Danegeld

Danegeld was an Anglo-Saxon form of taxation that predated the Norman conquest of England. It was also called the 'Heregeld' or 'The army tax'.

Initially it was a tax on land ownership that was used to provide funds to protect England against Viking raids and invasions. It was used by the Anglo-Saxons to pay for soldiers, to build fortifications and also used to buy off raiding Vikings with bribes.

William the Conqueror and his successors had used Danegeld to raise money but it had gradually been less used; King Stephen used the Danegeld only periodically.

Henry II revived the payment of Danegeld in 1155-6 but by 1161-2 at the latest he too had stopped collecting this tax. Danegeld fell out of favour under Henry II simply because it was an uneven and inefficient tax. It could only be used to tax those that owned land and people such as merchants and Jewish communities were untouched by the Danegeld.

The Danegeld was a tax that was issued on the whim of the king and so some years was not called for at all. Moreover, it did not take into calculation taxes on moveable property; which potentially could yield much greater results for the Exchequer.

Scutage

The word 'Scutage' literally means 'Shield Money' and is derived from the Latin word for shield – *'scutum'* and the implementation of scutum by King Henry II was an attempt to establish an orderly system of taxation.

What is Scutage?

According to the *Dialogus de Scaccario*;

"Occasionally it comes to pass that by the machinations of enemies the country is thrown into confusion and there is rebellion in the country. Then the king decrees that a certain sum be paid from each knight's fief, namely, a mark or a pound, whence come the pay and gratuities for the soldiers. For the prince prefers to thrust into the vortex of war mercenary troops rather than domestic forces. And so this sum is paid in the name of shields and is therefore called scutage."

Dialogus de Scaccario; Book 1. IX.

What was knight's service?

Knight's service was an obligation owed by a vassal to their lord in return for a tenancy of land.

If a baron owed the King 10 fees of knight's service he was required to send to the King 10 fully equipped and trained knights to serve in his army for a period of forty days.

How useful was Scutage?

Scutage was essentially a tax levied on knight's fees. It is first mentioned in 1100 as a tax that was levied on Church lands, the Church owned huge tracts of land in England in the 12th century and this property would otherwise be exempt from the provision of armed soldiers.

As a result the scutage was a tax that was designed to raise money. For each knight's fee scutage could instead be paid to the value of £3. The collection of the first scutage in England under King Henry II was in A.D. 1159.

It was really a commutation of military service in terms of a money payment, and was exacted from each knight's fief. Potentially the sums that could be gathered through Scutage were huge. Some medieval commentators assessed the number of knights' fees in England at 60,000 – a clear exaggeration.

In practice funds raised were much smaller, though still substantial. In 1159 Henry II invaded Toulouse, he raised an army for this siege using the scutage and raised some £9000 from scutage for this purpose – this would indicate that the number of knights' fees in 1159 at 3000.

Another scutage was raised in 1171 when Henry II invaded Ireland. On this occasion Henry II had an army of around 5-6000 men; only about 10% of whom were knights; the rest being mercenaries and feudal serjeants.

This money was used to pay for;

- Mercenaries
- siege engines
- supplies and transportation.

Cartae Baronum 1166

When Henry II became King in 1154, he could instruct his Exchequer to look to Domesday in order to see who owned what. However, a lot of time had passed since 1086.

Domesday needed updating. Henry II had decided that he would order a greater level of scrutiny of his tenants in chief. In 1166 he issued a command for all Earls and Barons to report to him. The result was the *Cartae Baronum;* 'the Baron's Certificates'.

In 1166 Henry II had been absent from England for some four years. Tenants-in-chief had been left alone to see to their own affairs, they had raised funds for themselves and spend it without the close eye of the king.

By 1166 Henry had been King of England for twelve years. He had faced border wars, rebellious vassals and had to assert his authority over his major tenants in chief and the King of Scotland. To a great degree he had succeeded in this, but running a kingdom was expensive and Henry II could never have access to enough money. He needed vast amounts of money to pay for his armies, to pay his servants, to keep his own house, to build his castles and palaces and to spend on diplomacy.

What was *Cartae Baronum?*

Cartae Baronum, the "Baron's Certificates", were reports sent by the barons and earls of England to Henry II.

They had been ordered to report the following;

- The amount of knights service owed by each baron and earl
- The names of their tenants that owed knight's service
- The sub tenancies that barons and earls and their families had created since the death of King Henry I in 1135.

According to the coronation charter of King Henry I, knight's service was specifically stated as an obligation by the king's vassals;

"To those knights who render military service for their lands I grant of my own gift that the lands of their demesne ploughs be free from all payments and all labour, so that, having been released from so great a burden, they may equip themselves well with horses and arms and be fully prepared for my service and the defence of my kingdom."

Responses to *Cartae Baronum*

There was a wide variety of style of response to *Cartae Baronum*. These took formal replies such as;

"This is the result of the enquiry which the Abbott of Ramsay made into the holdings of his knights at the King's command "

To personal, friendly responses;

"To his dear Lord Henry, King of the English, Hugh de Bayeux sends greetings. The old enfeoffments on my fief, namely on the day when King Henry your grandfather was alive and dead, are as follows..."

To the poverty claiming kind of response such as the one below;

"To his dearest Lord Henry King of the English, William son of Robert sends greeting. You should know that I hold of you the fief of one poor Knight; and I have not enfoeffed anyone on it since it is barely enough for me, and thus my father held it."

Why issue *Cartae Baronum?*

As a result King Henry II, by issuing *Cartae Baronum* in 1166, was trying to find out how many knights he could raise from his lords in England. However, there was more to it than this. It enabled him to more accurately assess how much money each lord was liable for, for taxation purposes.

In 1168 Henry II was to marry off his daughter Matilda. Since Henry II was required to provide a respectable dowry to accompany his daughter, perhaps *Cartae Baronum* was issued in order to raise funds to provide this cash dowry.

Another, more likely reason, for *Cartae Baronum* was to ensure that his tenants in chief were not trying to evade the responsibility of providing sufficient numbers of knights for Henry's armies.

A final reason for issuing *Cartae Baronum* was so that King Henry could raise money from his tenants-in-chief. Knights were liable for service for only forty days. In practice this would mean that any English knights that Henry wanted to use in his continental lands could only be used for a very limited amount of time. In practice a knight from Cumbria in Northern England could not be used in Aquitaine or Normandy since it would take too long for them to get there.

However, if Henry could get his tenants-in-chief to pay money in place of providing knight's service, he could then use this money to pay for mercenaries or to pay other knights to remain in action for a longer period of time and be able to conduct more sophisticated military operations such as the siege of Toulouse in 1159.

Task: Scutage, Danegeld and Cartae Baronum

Write a response to the following questions;

a) *How might taxes such as Scutage and Danegeld enable Henry II to extend his authority?*
b) *What shortcomings and problems might result from Danegeld and Scutage?*
c) *To what extent do you agree with the view that acts like Cartae Baronum and taxes like scutage gave Henry II's tenants-in-chief cause for resentment.*

Spend no more than 60 minutes on these questions

3.4 Law and order in 12th century England

In this section we will;

- *Explore the idea of Common Law*
- *Understand the Assizes of Clarendon of 1166*
- *Explore the significance of the Assizes of Clarendon of 1166*
- *Understand what Sheriffs were and what they did*
- *Understand what the Sheriff's Inquest was and its implications*
- *Consider the extent to which each office of state needed to work in unison*
- *Consider the role and function of Forest law*

Introduction

When Henry became King of England in 1154 he had a problem greater than any of his predecessors on the English throne. How could he effectively rule his vast domains? One group of officers of the land that Henry II relied upon was the Sheriffs.

What is Common Law?

The laws of the different lands and regions have a certain degree of variation. So for example the acts of murder or theft are generally considered to be illegal acts; acts that stand at odds with the generally acceptable rules of conduct in society.

Key term: Assize

legislation or a legal action.

When someone is suspected of commiting a crime such as murder or theft, they are judged by a set of procedures that are common to the country or region in which they are committed and judged. These common sets of procedures have evolved over a series of centuries.

Common law therefore is a standard set of procedures that are common across the region or kingdom.

Henry II contributed to our understanding and development of Common Law through a series of assizes – most prominently the major assizes of Clarendon in 1166 and Northampton in 1177 and the minor or 'petty' assizes of *Mort d'ancestor, Darrein presentment* and *novel disseisin.*

Assize of Clarendon

The Assize of Clarendon was a series of commands issued by King Henry II of England in a meeting of the *Concilium Curia Regis* at Clarendon in February 1166. The assize of Clarendon was an extreme attempt to control lawlessness.

The Assize of Clarendon was an attempt to improve and make more consistant procedures in criminal law. In it Henry II established across England juries consisting of twelve men in each *hundred* or four men in each town. The function of these juries was to inform the King's *itinerant judges* of the most serious crimes committed in the local area and to name *"any man accused or notoriously suspect of being a robber or murderer or thief."*

All men tried by the *itinerant judges* were subjected to ordeal by water and, if convicted, deprived of their goods and possessions, which were to be forfeited to the King. The result of this arrangement was that fines (*amercements*) resulting from these courts' judgements were to be paid into the Exchequer. Punishments could be harsh. A convicted man might have his foot amputated. Whilst even those found not guilty could be exiled from England if they were deemed to be men of ill repute. This was the fate of Becket's relatives. They had not committed a crime, but were exiled because they were tarnished by the actions of the Archbishop. As a result of actions such as the exile of Becket's family, the assize of Clarendon had the unfortunate effect of encouraging accusations which lead to miscarriages of justice.

Key terms

Hundred: An administrative subdivision of the country. There were approximately 650 Hundreds in England.

Eyre: A visit by the King's justices in a locality to deal with any judicial proceedings.

Itinerant Judges: Judges that tour the counties in the six judicial circuits.

Task: Examination style response

Read the following excerpt;

Below are three excerpts from the Assizes of Clarendon in 1166;

1. In the first place the said King Henry ordained on the advice of all his barons, for preserving peace and maintaining justice, that inquiry be made through the several counties and through the several hundreds by twelve more lawful men of the hundred and by four more lawful men of each vill, upon oath that they will tell the truth, whether in their hundred or in their vill there is any man cited or charged as himself being a robber or murderer or thief or anyone who has been a receiver of robbers or murderers or thieves since the lord king was king. And let the justices inquire this before themselves and the sheriffs before themselves.

7. And in the several counties where there are no jails, let them be made in a borough or in some castle of the king at the king's expense and from his wood if it is near, or from some neighbouring wood, on the estimation of the king's servants, to the end that the sheriffs may keep in them those who have been arrested by the officers whose function it is to do this and by their servants.

12. And if anyone be taken who has the spoil of his robbery or theft in his possession, if he bear an ill name and have a notoriously bad reputation, and have no warrant, let him not have law. But if he be not suspected on account of what he has in his possession, let him go to the water.

Write a response to each of the following questions;

a) Why is this source valuable to the historian for an enquiry into the organisation and function of law and order in England? Explain your answer using the source, the information given about it and your own knowledge of the historical context.

b) How much weight do you give to the evidence of this source for an enquiry into the authority of Henry II. Explain your answer using the source, the information given about it and your own knowledge of the historical context.

Spend no more than 45 minutes on this task

The Sheriffs – who were they and what did they do?

The Sheriffs were the chief officials and representatives of the king in the 38 Counties. Most Counties were under the control of a Sheriff and were responsible for enforcing the laws of the King.

The primary function of a Sheriff was to keep the King's peace and to enforce the law. The Sheriff however was also responsible for collecting the County Farm and amercements issued by local law courts. The Sheriff also was a source of law and order and justice. It was the Sheriff that was responsible for capturing outlaws, keeping and feeding prisoners, summoning jurors and installing them in a court of law as well as fining and executing criminals.

The Sheriff therefore had a dual function – enforcing the law and collection of taxes in the local area. Sheriffs were appointed by, and dismissed by, the King and were in theory independent of Barons and Earls. In practice many Sheriffs came from these same classes and therefore their own interests sometimes came into conflict with that of performing the office of Sheriff.

Sheriffs were usually resident in Royal Castles within the County for which they were responsible. Often this Royal Castle was within the centre of one of the major towns of the County. Lincoln Castle being a prime example as was Nottingham Castle.

Sheriff's Aid

The Sheriff of a County had wide-ranging duties. These duties cost money. Sheriff's Aid was a tax imposed upon Barons and Earls with land in a County that was payable directly to the Sheriff for the Sheriff to be able to cover the financial expense of covering his duties. In particular, Sheriffs required funds to be able to pay for the upkeep of his men at arms that would help him to keep order. Given that the Counties differed widely in size and population – Rutland, the smallest County was less than 5% the size of the largest; Yorkshire, the Sheriff's Aid and the expenses incurred by a Sheriff differed widely.

In 1163, King Henry II tried to adjust the way in which Sheriff's aid was collected and distributed. Henry II wanted the Sheriff's Aid paid directly into the Exchequer from which it could be distributed as required to the Sheriffs. This in effect would provide the Exchequer with additional income, but it would also ensure that the Sheriffs were more accountable for the money that they required. It would also cut down on corruption. As it was Sheriff's Aid was a tax that the sheriffs could quite easily manipulate and profit from.

In 1163 at the Council of Woodstock the newly appointed Archbishop of Canterbury Thomas Beckett refused to pay for Sheriff's Aid that was to go directly to the Exchequer. Beckett argued that the King was trying to take money from those who were in fact eligible for it and had relied upon this tax for generations.

This argument was one of the first between the two men over the relationship between the rights of the King and the rights of the lords of the land and the church.

1170 - The Inquest of the Sheriffs

In 1170 Henry had just returned to England after a period of several years when he was concerned primarily with his continental possessions. On his return to England in 1170 Henry II was determined to investigate the rumours he had received that his Sheriffs were not behaving as they ought. The result was the Sheriff's inquest.

The Inquest of Sheriffs resulted in most Sheriffs being removed from office; some 21 of the 28 sheriffs were sacked. New sheriffs were appointed both from poorer knightly families and from the wealthiest sections of society.

Alfred of Lincoln, was appointed the Sheriff of Dorset and Somerset and Alfred was a powerful man in the *Cartae Baronum.* Alfred had been assessed for being liable for some twenty five knights. Poorer Sheriffs included Hugh of Buckland, appointed Sheriff of Buckinghamshire and Oxfordshire. Hugh was a knight of few means, holding just one knight's fee according to the 1166 *Cartae Baronom.* Another family, the Estoutevilles, also benefitted from the Sheriff Inquest. Robert of Estouteville became Sheriff of Yorkshire, and his brother Roger was appointed Sheriff of Northumberland. The Estouteville brothers would as Sheriffs fight for Henry II in the Great Rebellion, being part of the army that captured King William the Lion of Scotland at Alnwick in 1174.

Another interesting individual was Ranulf de Glanvill. Ranulf de Glanville had been Sheriff of Yorkshire but was removed from this office in 1170. After proving his loyalty to King Henry II at the battle of Alnwick, Ranulf was re-appointed to the post of Sheriff of Yorkshire before becoming in time Justiciar of England in 1180.

The significance of the Sheriff Inquest

King Henry II was seeking men of ability and trust for this important post. It did not matter to him if his appointees came from the wealthiest sections of society. It is probable that most of the sheriffs sacked in 1170 may have been guilty of corruption or abuse of their office.

Task: King Henry II and the Sheriffs

Write responses to the following questions;

a) *How important do you think the office of Sheriff was to King Henry II?*
b) *In what ways do you think that the position of Sheriff could be a potential source of conflict between the King and his Earls and Barons?*

Spend no more than 30 minutes on these questions

Task: Examination style response

Read the following excerpt;

Excerpt from the Inquest of the Sheriffs 1170

In the first place the barons shall require security and pledge from all sheriffs who have been sheriffs since the lord king last crossed into Normandy, and from all who have been bailiffs or ministers of these [sheriffs], whatever bailiwick they have held from them; also from all those who since that time have held hundreds of the barons which they [the barons] have in the county, whether they have held them at firm or in custody;--that they will be before the lord king on the day which they [the barons] shall set for them for the purpose of doing right and redressing to him and his men what they ought to redress. . . .

Afterward they [the barons] shall take oath from all the barons and knights and free men of the county that they will tell the truth concerning that which shall be asked of them on behalf of the lord king; and that they will not conceal the truth for love of any one or for hatred or for money or reward or for fear or promise or for anything else.

Write a response to each of the following questions;

a) Why is this source valuable to the historian for an enquiry into the organisation and function of the office of the Sheriff?

Explain your answer using the source, the information given about it and your own knowledge of the historical context.

b) How much weight do you give to the evidence of this source for an enquiry into the workings of the office of Sheriff?

Explain your answer using the source, the information given about it and your own knowledge of the historical context.

The Royal Forest

Many forests were designated as 'Royal forests'; these areas of land provided food for the king and his court when it came into the region, but also sources of meat for his appointed officials in the region such as sheriffs and their men. Hunts also provided entertainment for the king and his court when they were within the area of a royal forest. Royal forests also provided income for the king, local peasants who used these woodlands to obtain timber and food could be taxed in return for this access.

In the 12th century, large parts (estimated at between a third or a quarter of the total land) of the country of England was defined as the 'Royal Forest'. Much of the Royal Forest was located in regions otherwise considered to be parts of baronial fiefs and the whole of Essex was part of the Royal Forest. Today, the New forest is a relic of the old Royal Forest.

Henry and the forest

According to the *Dialogus de Scaccario* the Royal Forest and the laws that governed it was described as;

"The whole organisation of the forests, the punishment, pecuniary or corporal, of forest offenses, is outside the jurisdiction of the other courts, and solely dependent on the decision of the king, or some officer specially appointed by him. The forest has its own laws, based...not on the Common law of the realm, but on the arbitrary legislation of the King".

In 1175 Henry II received details of a great forest eyre. This eyre was orchestrated by the chief forester Alan de Neville who had been tasked with restoring the boundaries of the Royal Forest in England to its' 1135 borders and to raise debts and fines worth a record £12,305 for Henry II. These fines in part came from abuses by the barons during the Great rebellion.

This Royal Forest was considered by the King to part of his own wealth and income and as a result income drawn from this source was paid direct to the Exchequer. The Royal Forest was a major source of the King's English revenue.

Alan de Neville

Alan de Neville was a minor noble from Lincolnshire. He was appointed chief forester by Henry II in 1166 at the Council of Clarendon and held this post until 1176. He was responsible for administering Royal Forest and courts that enforced forest law. De Neville was excommunicated by Thomas Becket on no fewer than two occasions for his support for the king and hostility towards Becket.

Legally, the Royal Forest was not subject to 'Common Law' and income raised from it could be raised arbitrarily by the will of the King. Revenue from the Royal Forest could take the following forms;

- Amercements (fines) - from those who poached wild animals from the Royal Forest such as deer, stags and boars.
- Purpresture – the construction of buildings within the Royal Forest
- Waste – tree felling within the Royal Forest
- Assart – land clearance for fields

Task: King Henry II and the Royal Forest

Write responses to the following questions;

a) How important do you think the Royal Forest was to King Henry II?
b) In what ways do you think that the Royal Forest could be a potential source of conflict between the King and his Earls and Barons?

Spend no more than 30 minutes on these questions

3.5 The State of England under Henry II

In this section we will;

- *Consider what England was like in the 12th century*
- *Understand the role and function of castles; civil and military*
- *Consider the extent to the necessity of castle building for Henry II in England*
- *Explore some case studies of castles*
- *Evaluate the extent to which castles preserved the integrity of the kingdom of England*

Introduction

In this section we will explore what England was like in the 12th century. We will also explore some of the main techniques used by Henry II to control and safeguard his lands. In particular we will explore Henry II's attitudes towards castles.

England during the 12th century

England was something of a backwater in comparison to the continent of Europe and in many ways England did indeed lag behind the rest of Europe. Windmills, for example had been used for centuries in mainland Europe, whereas in England the first recorded windmill dates only to 1180.

The population is hard to accurately assess. Estimates have ranged from between 1 million at the lowest end to as high as 5 million. In all probability the total population of England during the reign of King Henry II was probably between 2 and 3 million.

Much of England was covered in forests. Forests were crucial for the people of England. Forests provided not only extensive grounds for wild animals to live, but also provided the timber required for building materials, wood for fuelling fires and also provided land and income for the owners.

Other large areas of England were farmed for cereal crops and also for raising of livestock such as cattle, pigs, goats and sheep. Sheep provided meat, but especially wool, which was a valuable trading resource. Crops that were raised in England during the twelfth century included wheat, barley, oats, rye as well as beans and peas. Grain from England also was a tradable commodity and was exported to the continent. Grain was exported to Flanders and Norway whilst wool was exported to Flanders and Northern France.

The people of the Kingdom of England

In the twelfth century, the majority of the population of England was descended from Anglo-Saxon or peoples of Scandinavian origin, with a small number of groups of people identified as 'Britons'. Whilst the Anglo-Saxons occupied the bulk of southern and central regions of England, those of Scandinavian origin were located primarily in Yorkshire and Lincolnshire and along much of the eastern coast.

The Britons were located primarily in the western regions of England and also in Wales who had in origin descended from the British tribal groups that had been present in the British Isles when the Romans had invaded in the 1st century AD. Most of the population spoke English, but the bulk of the nobles of England had come much more recently from Normandy and France after the conquest in 1066.

These Anglo-Norman barons spoke French, with only a minority able to speak English with any fluency. There was then a disconnect between the nobles and the commons that was made wider by the fact that many of these lords did not consider themselves as originating in England and saw themselves as a separate ruling and ethnic class.

Towns and Cities

The major city of England then as now was London. It probably had a population of around 20,000 people – and was tiny in comparison to the great cities of Europe which included Cordoba in Spain and the capital of the Byzantine Empire, Constantinople (now modern day Istanbul in Turkey).

Other towns in England included cities such as York, Lincoln, Bristol and Exeter which probably had populations that did not exceed 10,000 inhabitants. Buildings in cities were usually built of wood and fires were commonplace. Streets in the cities and towns were little better than mud churned trails and inhabitants would also attempt to raise livestock such as pigs and cattle within their houses in these cities.

A pen portrait of London around 1170;

"...is fortunate in the wholesomeness of its climate, the devotion of its Christians, the strength of its fortifications, its well-situated location, the respectability of its citizens, and the propriety of their wives. Furthermore it takes great pleasure in its sports and is prolific in producing men of superior quality"

"there are also in London and in its suburbs thirteen conventual churches and one hundred and twenty six lesser, parish churches..."

"On the east side the royal fortress, of tremendous size and strength, whose walls and floors rise up from the deepest foundations – the mortar being mixed with animal's blood. On the west side are two heavily fortified castles. Running continuously around the north side is the city wall, high and wide, punctuated at intervals with turrets, and with seven double gated entranceways."

"Two miles from the city and linked to it by a populous suburb, there rises above the bank of that river the king's palace, a structure without equal, with inner and outer fortifications".

"To the north (of the city) there are tilled fields, pastures, and pleasant, level meadows with streams flowing through them, where watermill wheels turned by the current make a pleasing sound. Not far off spreads out a vast forest, its copses dense with foliage concealing wild animals – stags, does, boars and wild bulls."

"Every morning you can find (people) carrying on their various trades, those selling specific types of goods, and those who hire themselves out as labourers, each in their particular locations engaged in their tasks. Nor should I forget to mention that there is in London on the river bank amidst the ships, the wine for sale, and the store rooms for wine."

William FitzStephen writing in the 1170s

England and taxation

England however was extremely valuable to its rulers. This was because England was, by the standards of the time, well set up for the raising and extraction of taxes. English tax rates were higher than those that could be raised in most parts of Europe. This was possible because the Norman kings of England had maintained and built upon the tax system established by the Anglo-Saxon kings of England. For centuries before the reign of King Henry II, England had been subdivided into units of administration and taxation including;

- Counties
- Hundreds

Henry II therefore stood to gain much from a stable England that was at peace and able to yield unto its ruler a healthy supply of cash.

What are Castles?

Castles are fortified locations, places of safety where the inhabitants could take shelter in the event if an attack by an enemy. But they also fulfilled additional functions. Perhaps the first function of a castle that comes to mind was that of *defence*. A Castle with strong walls and towers provided a place of safety to which those who lived nearby could retreat to with their families and their property in the face of an attack by an enemy.

They were centres of *administration*, places where documentation and records could be kept safe. They would be central places from which local villagers and farmers could deliver their taxes to. They also could be used as places where courts could meet and settle disputes.

Castles were also centres for *observation and control*. This is perhaps the greatest role of a castle. By building a castle at a strategic location, for example on a hill overlooking a river crossing, or controlling a mountain pass in terrain which would be difficult or impossible to cross elsewhere, a castle could oversee who was passing through the area and soldiers from the castle could interrogate, oppose or harass any undesirable passing through the area.

A castle was also a *home* for a lord or his representative. The castle was an imposing construction that overarched and dominated the local area by its very appearance. It was therefore a suitable location for a lord to live. Some castles could be quite uncomfortable places to live for the majority of their inhabitants; however other castles could be opulent, even luxurious places to live. Difficult to access and secure; they also provided a safe haven for a lord to deposit his wealth in.

Castles in England

England has been described as a land of castles. The Norman conquerors of England after 1066 established castles throughout the country in order to keep themselves safe and to ensure that they could control their newly acquired lands. Indeed, on landing at Pevensey in 1066 the first act of William of Normandy was to construct himself a castle.

Castles in England

There were (and many still remain) lots of castles in England. Kings of England commonly used castle construction as a deliberate policy in order to increase the security and control their possessions.

Royal Castles, Baronial Castles and Illegal Castles

Henry II owned scores of castles across England. Those belonging directly to him were known as ***Royal Castles*** – often they were occupied in his name by Sheriffs and their men. Henry II of course, if he was in the area, would stay at these places and they would be places where Henry II could store treasure and war machines for use as required.

Other castles were constructed and owned by Barons and Earls. These were the ***'Baronial Castles'***. These were usually (though not always) less sophisticated the Royal Castles.

Case Study: Royal Castles

Scarborough Castle;

Scarborough Castle was constructed in the 1130s out of wood by the local Aumale family in order to protect Scarborough; a town that had a tradition of being attacked by sea raiders during the Viking period. In 1066, Scarborough had been sacked by Harald Hardrada on his way to his eventual defeat and death at the battle of Stamford Bridge.

Scarborough Castle was rebuilt in stone in 1150s after Henry II seized control of the place from the Aumale family. Henry II had the original castle declared as illegal (adulterine) and demolished, but recognised the strength of the location and the need for a castle here. The result was reconstruction. Between 1159-1169 Scarborough castle was rebuilt in stone and records suggest that the castle cost some £682 to build - £532 being spent between 1157-1164. This was a large amount of money to be spent on one location given than the total annual income of England was £22,000 at most under Henry II.

Dover Castle

Dover, like today, was an important port town and often seen as the gateway to the continent. Dover had been garrisoned since Roman times and William the Conqueror had constructed a castle here in 1066. It was therefore no surprise that Henry II would pay much attention to any castle built here.

In 1180 Henry II constructed a new castle at Dover. Part palace the castle at Dover was designed to be a strong place – a point of resistance to any planned invasion from across the Channel. Dover Castle was also built to impress and awe anyone who saw it.

In addition to being heavily fortified and protected with a sizeable garrison, the great tower was also a place of residence for the King, with personal quarters established on the top floor.

On the second floor of the great tower there was also built a shrine dedicated to Thomas Becket. In part this shrine was built as a point of pilgrimage for those pilgrims that were travelling to Canterbury to venerate the saint.

Still other castles were the ***'adulterine'*** or ***Illegal Castles***. One of the first actions of Henry II was to identify and demolish any castles that had been constructed illegally during the Anarchy.

Case Study: Baronial and illegal Castles

Wigmore Castle

Wigmore Castle in Herefordshire was first built in 1067 and since 1075 had been owned by the Mortimer family. Originally a Motte and Bailey construction, the castle was redesigned and rebuilt in stone in the early part of the 12th century. In 1155 when the Mortimer's resisted Henry II Wigmore was besieged by an army led by Henry II and forced to surrender. Thereafter the castle was restored to the control and ownership of the Mortimers.

Ongar Castle

Ongar Castle in Hampshire was built in the 12th century. A wooden construction in the form of a Motte and Bailey castle, it was probably constructed during the Anarchy. Possibly Ongar castle was initially identified as an illegal castle by Henry II. However in 1157 Ongar castle was granted to Richard de Luci (the future Justiciar) who then reconstructed the place in stone.

Newbury Castle

Newbury Castle was built by a minor noble called John Marshall to control the village of Hamstead Marshall and dates to 1152. It was an illegal construction and besieged by King Stephen. King Stephen threatened to execute John Marshall's second son – William Marshall in order to obtain the place. The bluff failed.

Task: Castles

Write a response to the following question;

To what extent do you agree with the view that King Henry II's main reason for owning castles in England was to ensure that the taxes continued to flow?

Spend no more than 30 minutes on this question

PART FOUR: Family and Rebellion

Part Four: Family and Rebellion

4.1 King Henry II and his family

4.2 The Great Rebellion

4.3 Henry II and the Papacy

4.4 Henry II and the extension of Royal Authority 1175-1182

4.5 Henry II: the final years 1185-1189

4.1 King Henry II and his family

In this section we will;

- *Explore the family of King Henry II*
- *Understand what advantages his family gave Henry II*
- *Consider the potential problems that could come from Henry II's family*
- *Understand the role of Henry the Young King and why he was a controversial figure*
- *Explore the extent to which Henry II utilised his family in order to achieve his own goals*

Introduction

King Henry II had a large family. In all he and his Queen Eleanor had no few than eight children together. King Henry II also had several illegitimate children.

The King and his children

Upon being crowned King of England in 1154, Henry II required a permament home for Queen Eleanor. He himself would need to continue to travel around his lands extensively, but the road was no place for a young family.

This permament home would not be in Aquitaine. Eleanor as we shall see was more loyal to Henry II when she was kept away from her ancestral homeland. So, Queen Eleanor would spend much of the 1150s and 1160s in England.

At first Eleanor dwelt in Westminster, and it was here that their second child was born. Henry was born on the 28th February 1155 and soon afterwards Eleanor was moved into a new palace at Bermondsey, just outside London. In 1156 the eldest child, William died, aged only three years old, but more children for the couple followed;

- Henry – February 1155
- Matilda – June 1156
- Richard – September 1157
- Geoffrey – September 1157
- Eleanor - 1161
- Joan - 1165

- John – December 1167

As the family grew so did the number of royal palaces in England for them to dwell at. New palaces were built at Clarendon and Woodstock in England early in Henry's reign and more locations were developed as royal residences later – such as at Oxford and Dover Castle.

Henry's sons

It is now time to explore the lives and early careers of Henry's sons. We shall overlook the tragically brief life of the eldest William, who was born in 1153 and died in June 1156. The other four sons of Henry survived to adulthood and three were crowned kings of England, although only two actually ruled. Two of Henry's sons predeceased Henry II.

Henry the Young King

Henry's Children

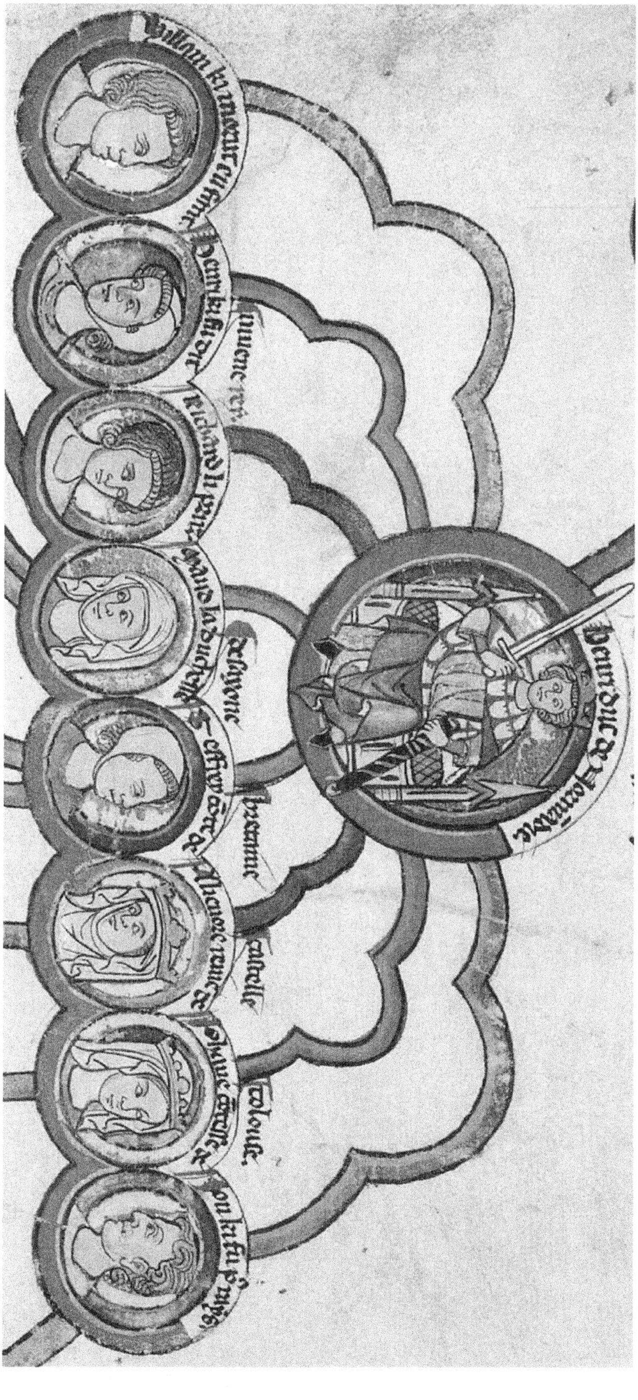

Henry the Young King

Henry the son of Henry and Eleanor was born in 1155 in England. He was the eldest son of Henry that grew to adulthood and was crowned by his father in a controversial ceremony in 1170. Controversiy surrounded the entire life of Henry 'the Young King'. His marriage was controversial, his coronation was controversial and his death was controversial. Henry never ruled as king despite being crowned one. This is why he is commonly called Henry the Young King as opposed to Henry III; who was a different man and a different king.

Early years

Beyond his birth, he first comes to the attention of historians when in 1160, aged five, Henry is married to Margaret, the two year old daughter of King Louis VII of France and his second wife Constanza of Castile.

This marriage was widely met with hostility from the Church. Neither child was able to take any degree of responsibility for their actions and neither would have been aware of the significance of the ceremony in which they took part. Despite this, the marriage was approved by both Henry II and Louis VII.

What was less weclome for Louis VII was the way in which the dowry of Margaret was seized by Henry II. Margaret's dowry was the region of land called the Vexin. This border region was along the eastern border of Normandy and a constant bone of contention between the French Kings and the Dukes of Normandy.

A King in training

In 1161 Henry was taken into the care and tutorage of Thomas Becket. However, when Becket argued with King Henry II, the young prince Henry was removed from the household of Becket. From an early age Henry was being groomed to become King. In 1162 the Exchequer records show that Henry II spent money on the purchase of a small crown and royal robes for his eldest son.

In 1162 and in 1163 young Prince Henry, now aged between seven and eight, received the homage of the English barons, Welsh princes and also the King of Scotland. In 1164, now aged eight, Henry was present and witnessed the Constitutions of Clarendon. The Constitutions were drawn up explicitly also to guarantee the rights of not just Henry II, but also his heir apparent.

A King in waiting

At the peace conference of Montmirail in January 1169, Henry II stated clearly his intentions to divide his inheritance up between his sons. Whilst Geoffrey would become Duke of Brittany, Richard would be Duke of Aquitaine and John at present, would receive nothing. The lion's share of the Angevin lands and inheritance would go to Prince Henry. Henry would receive the Kingdom of England, the Duchy of Normandy and the County of Anjou. In turn Henry's sons would give homage to King Louis VII of France. Henry then would in time become King and one of the most powerful rulers of Europe, but not yet. Henry II was still in his thirties, potentially then, Prince Henry would need to wait for several more decades at least before he could expect to become King.

A Controversial coronation

In June 1170 Prince Henry was aged fifteen and about to become a king. Henry II had wanted to crown his son earlier, but because of his argument with Becket, it had not been traditionally possible for a coronation to be performed in England.

However, Henry II had decided that it was time his son was crowned. Henry II had convinced the Archbishop of York to perform the ceromony in Westminster Abbey in the presence of at least ten bishops and on June 14th the coronation took place. For the first time since the 9th century, England had more than one crowned King.

In order to prevent possible disruption and interference by either the exiled Archbishop of Canterbury or the Pope, Henry II had ordered a lockdown of all ports in England in order to ensure they could not prevent the coronation. King Henry and Queen Eleanor witnessed their son's coronation with many others, but absent from proceedings was Henry the Young King's wife Margaret; she remained in Normandy. Perhaps she was prevented from reaching England through bad weather. More likely it was a deliberate snub to her and her father; the French king.

Not only then had Henry had his son crowned against the traditional customs of England, the coronation took place without Margaret. Young Henry might be a King of England now, but his wife was not yet Queen.

A King without power?

Henry the Young King was now *'rex designatus'* and as such received a King's seal. However; this seal was only one sided. Henry II and all other Kings of England possessed double sided seals. Henry the Young King's seal also lacked the inclusion of a sword in the engraving. This was a sign that young Henry lacked full authority and was very much the junior partner.

Henry II also appointed his son's advisors and most of his household knights. This could be seen as a sensible precaution. Henry was only fifteen after all and still a boy, one of these retainers was William Marshall, who was to instruct Henry in theart of being a knight. These experienced men would help advise Henry the Young King, but they were first and foremost Henry II's chosen men. They would act in his best interests, or so he hoped. Henry II departed shortly after the coronation to return to Normandy, leaving his son in charge in England.

Henry II was embroiled in illness and controversy for the remainder of 1170. In August 1170 Henry II was struck down by a serious illness. For a month or so the King lay near death and preperations were made in England to have Henry the Young King ready to succeed his father. However the danger passed and Henry II, in gratitude for his recovery conducted a three hundred mile pilgrimage from September to November 1170 to the shrine of the Virgin Mary at Rocamadour in southern Aquitaine.

Henry II's troubles were not over however. With the controversy of the murder of Thomas Becket within months of the coronation saw

Henry II widely unpopular and discredited amongst the Church and amongst the peasantry of England. Henry the Young King would remain in charge of England until the summer of 1172, when Henry finally returned to England. In this time Henry the Young King seems to have ensured that England remained stable and calm.

Despite this evidence that Henry the Young King could rule with a steady hand in the absence or sickness of King Henry II, he was becoming increasingly frustrated that he held no real power In 1173 Henry the Young King would challenge his father.

The Young King's second coronation

Whilst his father was in Ireland, Henry the Young King crossed to Normandy to hold his Christmas court there in 1171-1172. In doing so, Henry was reunited with is wife Margaret but her absence at the coronation still rankled with King Louis VII and no doubt with her.

Aged seventeen, Henry the Young King returned to England to a reunion with his father. In August 1172, the Archbishop of Rouen performed a second coronation of the Young King at Winchester, this time with Margaret at his side.

Henry Lackland?

Technically, the Young King should have had possession of the Vexin region now, after all that region had been the dowry of Margaret back in 1160. However despite being granted a large cash subsidy, King Henry II still refused to give his son any direct control over lands. The Young King had obligations to fulfil. He had his own retinue of advisors and knights and these men looked to the Young King for rewards and for lands and titles. Henry the Young King however had none to give.

This refusal to grant his son any independence was increasing resentment. According to the contemporary chronciler Walter Map Henry II had learned this tactic from his mother Matilda. It was according to Map, Henry II's way *'to acquire loyalty through the denial of favour'*. It seems that Henry II had noticed the possibility of this resentment; he stripped several of his son's advisors and friends from his service.

Task: Henry the Young King

Historians have differed in their judgment of Henry the Young King. For example;

Prof. Lewis Warren (1973) argued that Henry the Young King was shallow, vain, careless, irresponsible and incompetent.

Dr Thomas Asbridge (2015) argues that Henry II was a politically able and engaged member of the Angevin dynasty.

From what we have seen of Henry the Young King's life and career to 1172 which of these judgements do you think is the more accurate? Write a paragraph or two that explains your reasoning.

Spend no more than 15 minutes on this question

Richard: A brief introduction

Richard was the second eldest surviving son of Henry II. Richard was born on the 8th September 1157 at Oxford in England. Despite being born in England Richard spent much of his childhood in Aquitaine and it seems that from a very early age Henry II had decided that Richard would become the future Duke of Aquitaine.

Aged twelve, Richard was confirmed as the future Duke of Aquitaine at the Conference of Montmirail by his father and also by Louis VII. At Montmirail it was also agreed that Richard would marry Alice, the king's daughter by his second wife.

In 1173, aged sixteen, Richard joined the Great Rebellion against his father but was rapidly defeated and forced to surrender. Thereafter Richard became increasingly more difficult for his father to control, fighting against his elder brother the Young King in 1182 after the Young King tried to exert his authority over Aquitaine.

On the death of Henry the Young King in 1183, Richard became Henry II's heir, but being heir apparent did not improve relations between Henry II and Richard. In 1187 Richard demonstrated his headstrong nature by taking the Cross before his father after the capture of Jerusalem by Saladin. Then in 1188-1189 Richard rebelled against Henry II and fought him until a peace was arranged a few days before the death of Henry II.

Geoffrey: A brief introduction

Geoffrey was born almost a year after Richard, in September 1158. Geoffrey was rapidly chosen by his father to become Duke of Brittany when he was married to Constance of Brittany in 1163. Geoffrey was aged five, Constance aged eight.

In 1173 Geoffrey, aged fifteen joined the Great Rebellion against Henry II but like his brothers rapidly brought to heel. Thereafter Geoffrey seems to have supported his eldest brother Henry and in 1182, sided with the Young King against Richard. In 1183 Geoffrey even arranged to assassinate his father but was again brought to heel. In 1184 Geoffrey demanded that since the Young King was dead, he should become Count of Anjou once Henry II died. Henry II refused and Geoffrey deserted his lands and went to Paris and the French court. At the French Court Geoffrey seems to have spent his time in feasting and tournaments and it was in a tournament in 1186 that he was killed, trampled to death by horses.

John: A brief introduction

John was the youngest son of Henry II and born on Christmas Eve 1167. John seems to have been raised and tutored by his eldest brother Henry and also by the Justiciar of England, Ranulf Glanvil.

John was nicknamed in his youth as 'lackland', because Henry II had made no provision for his youngest son at the Conference of Montmirail. However, John would marry Isabelle de Clare and acquire through this marriage substantial estates in England, Wales and Ireland. In 1184 John remained loyal to his father against Richard over Aquitaine and in 1185 John was sent to Ireland to rule their as 'Lord of Ireland'. Within six months he and his chief retainers would succeed in alienating the Irish and encourage rebellion against him.

Thereafter John remained loyal to his father until in 1189, when rumours reached Henry II already mortally sick, that John had joined his brother Richard and betrayed him. John would succeed as King of England in 1199 after the death of his brother Richard the Lionheart.

Medieval Princesses

> ***Key terms***
>
> ***Dowry** – a 'bride price'.*
>
> *A dowry is a gift of money or land that is gifted by the family of the bride to the husband when they are married.*
>
> *A dowry had to be suitable for the rank and wealth of the daughter. So the richer and more powerful the father, the more expensive the dowry of the daughter.*
>
> ***Usurp** – to successfully overthrow the ruler.*

In Medieval Europe the daughter of a King was both a potentially valuable asset to the ruler, but they were also potentially an expensive asset and could even be a potential threat.

For each female child that a medieval king or lord had, they had to take into consideration the following strategies and weigh up the pros and cons of each;

- Marry daughter to a suitable husband amongst your own supporters
- Confine daughter to a nunnery
- Marry daughter to a suitable husband outside of your authority
- Marry your daughter to your enemy

Marry the princess to a suitable husband among your own supporters

A suitable husband was a man of equal or near equal rank. They could be another King or Lord who already had wealth, possessions and power, or the son of a great lord who could potentially in time inherit. If this husband was one of your own tenants in chief – such as Duke or Earl for example, as king you would be favouring this man with additional prestige and additional land and or wealth through the dowry.

A major potential problem with this strategy would be that you would be creating a tie of marriage with the royal family to the family of your supporter. In the future this might mean that the supporter's family would have a link to the throne and could even encourage them to try to usurp you. A ruler who married his daughter to one of his own supporters also enriched the new husband by giving a dowry. In the case of great lords, this dowry was often large amounts of land.

Confine daughter to a Nunnery

This option sounds harsh. But what if a lord or king cannot find a suitable husband for his daughter? What if he cannot or does not want to provide a dowry? What if the only option for a husband is a merchant or lowly landless knight?

In this case the lord might simply decide that his daughter is better off not being married. If she is sent to a religious institution, the daughter will be educated and may become a person of authority in the Church. The Church may be more sympathetic to a ruler that demonstrates their piety by offering one of their beloved children to the service of the Church.

Marry daughter to a suitable husband outside of your authority

12th century Europe was a large place with many lords and kings. At any one time a large number of these men were unmarried and potential husbands for the daughter of another great lord.

A ruler or great lord that chose a husband from outside his authority was able to establish strong links with another ruler or lord. This lord could then be a potential ally against another rival lord; by marrying your daughter to a lord outside of your own authority you could also use the occasion to create new alliances or disrupt established alliances. A sizeable dowry could be a small price to pay for a valuable new alliance.

One downside of such a strategy was that you might never see your daughter again. Another potential problem was that you might in time have a distant family with a strong claim to your own lands through this marriage.

Marry your daughter to your enemy

Another possible option for a ruler or lord was to marry your daughter into the family of your enemy. By doing so you might end the conflict and your enemy cease to be your enemy. Alternatively the marriage could result in giving your enemy greater claim and ammunition to use against you in the event of an unforeseen accident or scandal.

The dowry given to an enemy could also be problematic. You might want the land and money back in time, this dowry could also make you poorer financially or territorially; and you will have given this wealth to your enemy.

Henry's daughters

Henry II had three daughters as well as four sons; Matilda, Joan and Eleanor. Given that Henry had many sons, these daughters were never considered by Henry II as likely candidates to succeed to the throne of England; however Henry II was man that liked to see his children earn their keep.

Henry arranged marriages for all three daughters;

Matilda married Duke Henry of Saxony, a great lord in Germany and also a major rival of the Emperor Frederick Barbarossa.

Joan married King William II of Sicily; a wealthy island kingdom in the Mediterranean, and a major port of departure for those headed to Palestine.

Eleanor married King Alfonso of Castile, the most power Christian kingdom in Spain.

All three marriages have common themes that can instruct us into Henry II's decision to enter into them. All three daughters were married to kings or effective rulers in their own right. All three marriages were to men far removed from Henry II's own lands and territories. All three marriages were to lords whose lands were closer in proximity to the lands of the French King Louis VII than they were to Henry's own lands.

It is interesting that Henry elected not to marry any of his daughters to any French lord, or into the French royal family. King Louis VII of France did not have a son until 1165, but Joan for example was born around the same time. Henry II then was determined that none of his daughters and none of his lands or wealth in the form of a dowry should find its way into the control or authority of the French crown.

The marriages of Henry II's sons

Unlike his daughters, Henry II was quite happy to arrange marriages between his sons and French princesses. Henry II was eager to have most of his sons married at an early age. In doing so he would acquire dowries and secure political advantage, not just for his children, but for himself as he effectively governed these lands himself.

In 1160 for example Henry II arranged the marriage of his son and heir Henry to Margaret, the daughter of King Louis VII of France and received as a dowry the Vexin region.

Before Henry's marriage to Margaret, Henry had already arranged a marriage between his third son Geoffrey (born in 1158) to the three year old daughter of Duke Conan of Brittany. When Duke Conan called in Henry II to help him fight a rebellion in 1166, Henry II had Conan stripped of his Duchy and installed himself in his place, acting as guardian for Geoffrey who was not even ten years old.

In 1169 at the Conference of Montmirail; Louis VII agreed to marry his daughter Alice to Henry II's second eldest son Richard in return for an act of homage for the Duchy of Aquitaine. The marriage of Alice and Richard never went ahead but the intention was there.

Finally in 1175 Henry II arranged the marriage of his youngest son John to Isabelle de Clare, the daughter of Strongbow, the man who had conquered large amounts of Ireland. Strongbow had no sons and so by marrying Isabelle to John, Henry II was able to provide lands in Ireland to his youngest son, who now took the title 'Lord of Ireland'.

Task: Henry II and the use of marriage alliances

Henry II achieved more power through the marriages of his children than he did through military power.

To what extent do you agree with this view?

Write a response to this question in no more than 500 words

4.2 The Great Rebellion 1173-1174

In this section we will;

- *Explore the roots of the Great Rebellion*
- *Consider the potential problems that could come from Henry II's family*
- *Understand the role of Henry the Young King and why he was a controversial figure*
- *Consider the extent to which Henry II's own actions drove his family and others to rebel*

Introduction

In the years 1172 to 1174 Henry II was confronted by a massive and co-ordinated rebellion across his lands. From Aquitaine to Scotland Henry II and his supporters fought a series of wars against his rebellious subjects and their allies from neighbouring lands.

In this section we will explore origins of this so called 'Great Rebellion' who supported the rebellion and the motives of those that chose to rebel against him.

The meeting at Limoges

In November 1172 Henry the Young King and his wife travelled to Paris and the court of Louis VII. Officially the visit was ceremonial but future events suggest that Louis VII began to encourage Henry to rebel against his father.

On the 25th of February 1173 Henry II ordered his sons to attend him at a family conference. Present were Henry II, Queen Eleanor, Henry the Young King, Richard, Geoffrey and John. Also in attendance were many lords including the Count of Toulouse.

Henry II announced at this conference that his son John (aged six) would marry the daughter of a French Count. Not only would the boy John gain a wife, he would also gain possession of three castles; Loudon, Mirebeau and Chinon, all three of which were in the County of Anjou. Not everyone was pleased.

Henry the Young King's motives for rebellion

Henry the Young King was among those unhappy by these events. The three castles were part of the property of the Count of Anjou, and the Young King was the future Count of Anjou. The Young King angrily rejected this decision and confronted his father.

It seems that Henry the Young King was heavily in debt by 1173, now eighteen years old he had come of age but stilled lacked any land beyond that given by his father to fund the lifestyle and retinue of a king in waiting.

The Young King demanded that Henry II immediately surrender up to him the County of Anjou, the Duchy of Normandy or the Kingdom of England. Henry II refused.

Task: Henry the Young King revisited

In the previous section we explored the views of two Historians with differing opinions of Henry the Young King.

Professor Lewis Warren (1973) argued that Henry the Young King was shallow, vain, careless, irresponsible and incompetent.

Dr Thomas Asbridge (2015) argues that Henry II was a politically able and engaged member of the Angevin dynasty.

From what we have seen of Henry the Young King's life and career to the year 1173 which of these judgements do you think is the more accurate? Has your view of Henry the Young King changed?

Write a paragraph or two that explains your reasoning.

Spend no more than 15 minutes on this question

Paris: Spring 1173

At Limoges, the Count of Toulouse approached Henry II and informed him that Henry the Young King, Richard and Geoffrey were all conspiring with their mother to rebel against him. Henry II did not want to believe this information. He announced that he would be heading north. Henry II requested the Young King to accompany him; the other sons would be left in the care of their mother in Aquitaine. The Young King was in a form of house arrest. Henry II also quietly alerted the commanders of his Royal castles through Anjou, Normandy and Aquitaine to begin preparation for war.

A few weeks later in April 1173 Henry the Young King escaped from Chinon castle with most of his household, but Margaret was left behind. The Young King made his way to Paris and the court of Louis VII which he reached in the spring of 1173.Henry the Young King was joined at Paris by his brothers Richard and Geoffrey. Queen Eleanor too, tried to reach Paris but was detained by Henry II's men and held in house arrest for the duration of the rebellion.

Henry II sent an embassy to Paris to order the return of his sons and also to inquire as to the intentions of the French King. In the presence of this embassy King Louis VII proclaimed Henry the Young King as sole Henry King of England. The message was clear. Henry II's crown was under threat and war was inevitable.

King Louis VII provided Henry the Young King with the paraphernalia of royalty. He was given robes of state and issued with a Royal Seal. In order to receive recognition from a higher power; the conspirators sent an embassy to the Pope in order to obtain his support.

The Rebels

Henry the Young King and King Louis VII recruited an impressive number of willing lords to their cause. The most prominent were;

- King Louis of France
- Henry the Young King
- Richard, son of Henry II
- Geoffrey, son of Henry II
- William the Lion, King of Scotland
- Philip, the Count of Flanders
- Theobald, Count of Blois
- Mathew, Count of Boulogne
- Robert, Earl of Leicester
- Hugh Bigod, Earl of Norfolk
- The Earl of Chester
- The Bishop of Durham

The motives of the opposition

As a list of enemies this was quite impressive. Many of them had much in common. The sons of Henry II were young and eager, but inexperienced in war, as was the case for Earl of Leicester and Mathew of Boulogne. Richard had experienced some warfare in Aquitaine subduing rebellious lords, but aged only fifteen he could hardly be regarded as a grizzled veteran. All were eager to acquire land and wealth by depriving Henry II of these same commodities. Some of the English Earls and Barons that joined the rebellion had been stripped of lands and estates by Henry II and the tightening up of regulations had increased income into the Exchequer but reduced the amount going directly to his tenants in chief.

Henry the Young King used his Royal seal liberally to dispense title and lands to those now rallying to his support. For example;

- William the Lion, King of Scotland was granted possession of the Counties of Cumberland and Northumberland.
- Philip, Count of Flanders was appointed the Earl of Kent and received the castles of Dover and Rochester.
- Theobald, Count of Blois was granted lands in Touraine and promised money from the revenues of Anjou.

The role of Queen Eleanor

Queen Eleanor had intended to join her sons at Paris in the spring of 1173, but Henry II was able to successfully capture and detain his wife.

Why might Eleanor have been willing to join the conspiracy against her husband? Some historians of the 19th century argued that Eleanor was offended that her husband had replaced her in the bedroom with a younger rival named Rosamund Clifford. We can discount this as a major motive, Henry II seems to have had several mistresses scattered across his lands, with the result that he had several illegitimate children. Some of these children were now young men; one was a Bishop in England who took part in the fighting during 1173-4.

Eleanor had been kept in England and Normandy for decades, only briefly permitted to visit her native Duchy of Aquitaine on certain occasions. After 1167, Eleanor was increasingly resident in Aquitaine and concerned that her tenants in chief looked to Henry II for leadership and authority; not her.

Now that she was home, Eleanor had increasingly become concerned that her own authority in Aquitaine was being eroded by Henry II's actions. Henry II had and would grant away lands and titles in Aquitaine to those he saw fit. He had punished the Lusignan family and also the Counts of Angouleme and La Marche for their rebellion in the 1160s and a typical punishment for rebels was to have some or all of their lands and territories removed and reissued to others. Henry II used England to raise vast income for himself, Aquitaine was undergoing similar treatment.

Eleanor was also concerned about the future role of her son Richard. Henry II had appointed Richard as the future Duke of Aquitaine at Montmirail in 1169. However, Henry II was impinging on Richard's rights in this position. For example Henry II had recently requested that the Count of Toulouse give homage to Henry the Young King for his estates in Aquitaine. Technically, The Count of Toulouse should have given this homage to Richard. In 1177, after the Great Rebellion, Henry's daughter Eleanor would be married to Alfonso of Castile. Her dowry would be the County of Gascony. This arrangement was probably already being planned before 1173 as it would require some detailed legislation and reorganisation.

Eleanor and Richard then had a motive to rebel against Henry II. Their main motive was to protect their respective rights in the Duchy of Aquitaine.

> ***Medieval Source Excerpts***
>
> *At the end of this study guide in Appendix 1, Document 3 is presented selected excerpts from the contemporary writer Roger of Hovedon's account of the Great Rebellion.*

Henry II's preparations

Given the number of threats against Henry II in 1173 he needed to remain largely on the defensive initially. At least on the Continent in this Henry II had a major advantage; his forces would be primarily based in Normandy and Anjou; from this central position he could attack or defend from attacks that could not necessarily support each other if co-ordination was lacking.

Possible attacks could come from a variety of locations and varying in severity;

- An attack by the Scots against Northern England
- Cross Channel invasions by the Counts of Flanders and Boulogne
- Rebellion in England by English Earls and Barons
- A border war with the Welsh
- Invasions of Normandy and Anjou by French armies
- Rebellion in Brittany
- Rebellion in Aquitaine

One advantage Henry II did have was that he was cash rich; much wealthier than all of his opponents combined. Henry II also had established contacts with a wide number of mercenary outfits and he once again ensured that these mercenaries were recruited to his side at rates of pay that others could not match. Money was made available to Richard de Luci, his Justiciar in England who was able to recruit a sizeable force with money taken from the Exchequer.

Henry II himself moved to Normandy and prepared two armies. One to invade Brittany and the principal force – which Henry II himself commanded to defend Normandy against attacks on his eastern frontier.

The Great Rebellion: fighting in Normandy and Brittany 1173

In April and May 1173 King Louis VII and Henry the Young King began a series of border raids on Normandy. These attacks met prepared opposition and rapidly retired, but the pair returned in June with a larger army and captured Aumele and Driecourt. At Driecourt however the Count of Boulogne was killed and the opposition to Henry II lost its first important individual.

Simultaneously, Richard and Geoffrey raised rebel forces in Aquitaine and Brittany, but they did not receive wholehearted support. Both regions were soon disrupted by civil war.

Henry II sent an army into Brittany to deal with Geoffrey and his supporters, whilst he led a larger army against Louis VII and the Young King. Henry II's armies were largely composed of experienced mercenaries who though expensive to maintain, were much more useful in warfare than the raised levies of inexperienced soldiers used by Louis VII.

No major battles were fought on the continent in the summer of 1173 but Louis VII and the Young King were forced out of Normandy. In Brittany, Geoffrey's supporters wavered. Given the choice between an inexperienced boy and the most powerful man in Western Europe many would-be rebels now began to see the positives of the latter; especially when his bloodthirsty and rapacious mercenaries were in the area.

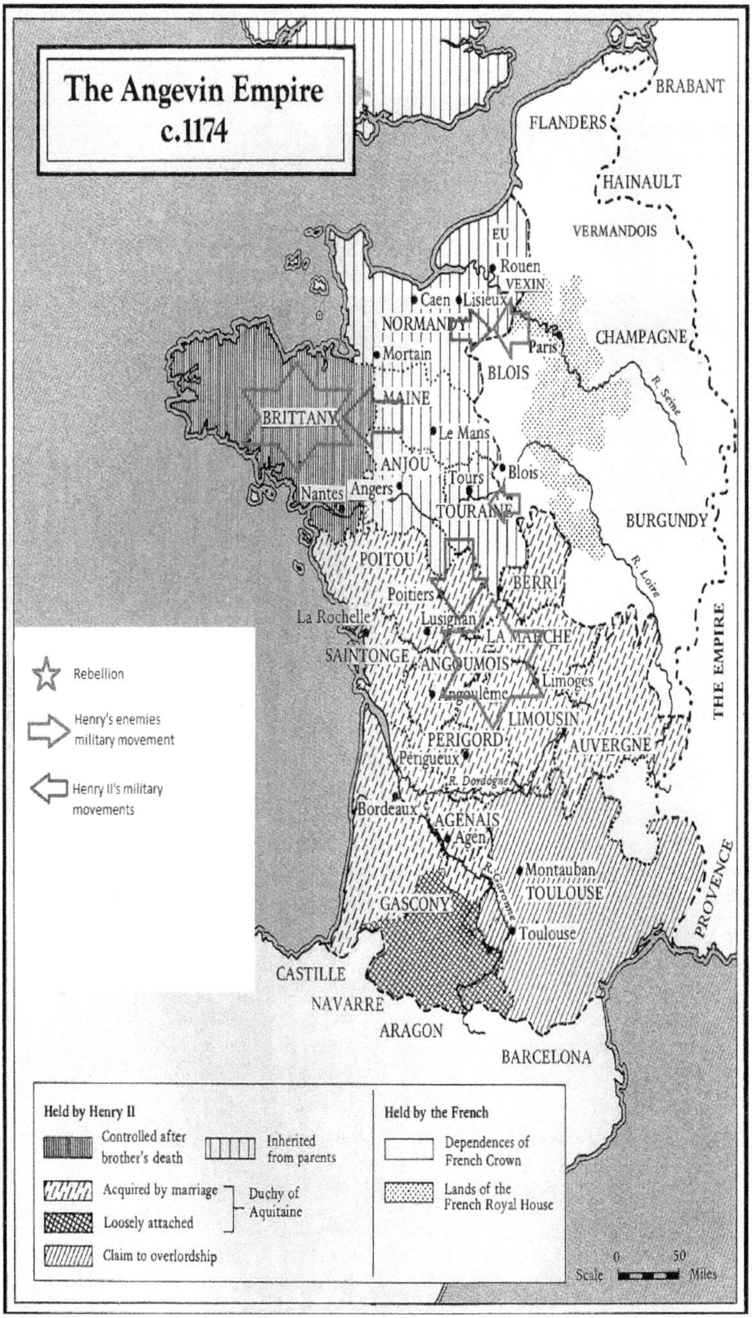
The Angevin Empire
c.1174
BRABANT
FLANDERS
HAINAULT
VERMANDOIS
EU
Rouen
VEXIN
Caen
Lisieux
NORMANDY
Paris
CHAMPAGNE
Mortain
BLOIS
R. Seine
MAINE
BRITTANY
Le Mans
ANJOU
Tours
Blois
Nantes
Angers
TOURAINE
BURGUNDY
POITOU
R. Loire
BERRI
Poitiers
La Rochelle
Lusignan
LA MARCHE
SAINTONGE
ANGOUMOIS
Limoges
Angoulême
LIMOUSIN
PERIGORD
AUVERGNE
Périgueux
R. Dordogne
Bordeaux
AGENAIS
Agen
Montauban
TOULOUSE
GASCONY
R. Garonne
Toulouse
PROVENCE
THE EMPIRE
CASTILLE
NAVARRE
ARAGON
BARCELONA
Rebellion
Henry's enemies military movement
Henry II's military movements
Held by Henry II
Controlled after brother's death
Inherited from parents
Acquired by marriage
Loosely attached
Duchy of Aquitaine
Claim to overlordship
Held by the French
Dependences of French Crown
Lands of the French Royal House
Scale 0 50 Miles

Gisors 1173

Already Louis VII was considering peace, perhaps his heart had never really been in the whole affair. A conference at Gisors was arranged but failed to come to terms when the Earl of Leicester began to shout abuse at Henry II. Robert the Earl of Leicester was the son of Henry's first Justiciar and one reason why he was so motivated against Henry II was that he felt that he had not been given an important and lucrative position in government like his father had been.

The rebellion in England 1173

In England he rebellion flared up in 1173 and through much of 1174. Here Henry II was absent in 1173 and therefore he was utterly reliant upon his chosen representatives. If these men proved to be unreliable then England could potentially be lost for Henry II before he could return and stabilise the situation.

Fortunately for Henry II, his main representatives were well chosen, men of proven ability. The Scottish army of William the Lion invaded Northern England in 1173 and at the same time several Earls rebelled in England.

William the Lion's army ravished Northern England, but the Justiciar Richard de Lacy gathered an army together and counterattacked in turn. Whilst the Scottish forces raided and besieged castles at Carlisle and Prudhoe, Richard de Lacy attacked and captured the Scottish held town of Berwick, then fell back south to deal with Richard, Earl of Leicester and Earl Bigod.

At the battle of Fornham in the Midlands; the loyalist forces of de Lacy defeated Leicester was defeated in battle and captured. Local peasants joined in the attacks on the rebel Earls and hunted them across the fields.

However, Hugh Bigod rallied his forces and recruited mercenaries from the Continent. The loyalist forces were defeated in a series of battles across the Midlands. If the rebellion in England was to be defeated, Henry II would need to come and help.

The rebellion in Aquitaine 1174

In Early 1174 Henry II had stabilised the situation in Brittany and along the Normandy border. He now led his army south against Aquitaine were his son Richard was in command.

Henry II's army was aggressive. Much of Northern Aquitaine was raided. The towns of Saintes and Taillebourf were captured and the area around Poitiers; Richard's base of power was devastated. Richard would in the future become one of the military greats of the 12th century. Here and now he was received a good education from his father on how to make an opposing lord look powerless.

To do the unexpected

In Northern France the Young King and Philip Count of Flanders were preparing an invasion fleet, planning to attack and occupy England. Henry II needed now to get to England first.

Heading north from Aquitaine, Henry II embarked an army and sailed in stormy weather to England. With him he took Queen Eleanor and Margaret. These women were too valuable to be left out of his sight in such difficult times.

Henry landed in Southampton in late June 1174. Despite the actions of Richard de Lacy and Henry's loyal supporters, his position in England was precarious. William the Lion was still attacking Northern England and besieging castles roughly along the line of Hadrian's Wall. The earls of Chester and Norfolk had raised their forces and were raiding the midlands and an invasion by the forces of the Count of Flanders seemed imminent.

Militarily then, Henry II should have headed north from Southampton. But he didn't. He travelled east, to Canterbury. Henry II rode to within sight of Canterbury cathedral and then dismounted and took off his shoes.

The Penance of Henry II

In a public display in July 1174, Henry II walked barefoot several miles to Canterbury Cathedral and entering the Cathedral threw himself before the tomb of Thomas Becket and was publically whipped by the assembled bishops and priests in order to atone. Before the tomb Henry II lay prostrate for a full day and a night begging forgiveness from the murdered Archbishop.

The penance seems to have had the desired results. On the 12th July 1174 William the Lion had been captured in battle at Alnwick by the Sheriff of Yorkshire Ranulf de Glanvil. The Scottish armies retreated northwards as news came that Henry II was heading towards them.

Henry II, invigorated by his public scourging and the news of William the Lion's capture, conducted a whirlwind tour of retribution across the lands of his traitorous Earls before returning to Normandy in August 1174.

Rouen 1174

Hearing that Henry II had crossed to England before them, the Young King and the Count of Flanders abandoned their plans to cross to England. Instead, the pair joined with the King of France in a new invasion of Normandy. The capital Rouen was besieged by their armies.

Henry II received the news of the siege of Rouen in August 1174. He was in England but rapidly crossed back to Normandy to confront the enemy and end the siege.

Once again, when confronted with the prospect of a face to face encounter with Henry II, Louis VII seemed to blanch. After some skirmishing between the two forces, Louis VII ordered the end of the siege and retreated. Henry II pursued and cut up the stragglers.

Peace

Almost everywhere, Henry II had emerged from the Great Rebellion victorious. William the Lion was captured; the Count of Boulogne was dead. There were still flickers of rebellion; Geoffrey and Richard were still defiant, but they were effectively confined. Henry the Young King still lacked his own powerbase and Louis VII never really seems to have had his heart in the whole enterprise and the Counts Blois and Flanders might face an invasion in turn.

At Montlouis in September 1174 a peace conference was arranged and all the major continental protagonists were present. Some willing – like Louis VII, others more reluctant, like Richard.

The peace agreed was that all sides would return their conquests. Prisoners would be released (with the exception of William the Lion) and Henry II's sons would be reinstated in their positions.

In addition each son would receive additional income;

Richard and Geoffrey would each get half of the incomes of their own Duchies, formerly all the income had gone to Henry II. John would receive the three castles of Loudon, Mirebeau and Chinon in Anjou and the Young King would receive direct ownership of two castles in Normandy and an annual income of £15,000 – an immense sum.

Task: Examination style response

The penance of Henry II 1174

On the guilt of Henry II and subsequent public penance for the murder of Archbishop Becket;

"Because however you asked about the death of the blessed martyr Thomas, I say in the word of the Lord and in the order of deacon to you, that in conscience I believe in no way that the king was guilty of this thing; and the most complete confirmation of this the lord Theodinus, bishop of San Vitale and the lord Albert the chancellor [the future Pope Gregory VIII] will make to you, who because of this matter investigated in our regions performing the office of legate; they confirmed the innocence of the man: and also they will assure you that this deed was done by certain men under his shadow, that all this iniquity came out from the sanctuary. For in fact, the canonical purgation having been accepted by them, they pronounced a judgment publicly by order of the highest pontiff, that he was free of this crime before God and men, and they bent back the mark of infamy on those very magnates, whose malice they had clearly proven in this matter."

"Also you will have learned that the lord king has made the glorious martyr his chief patron in all his needs. For in fact on the very day when he first visited the tomb of the martyr, he subjected the king of Scots, persecutor and attacker most strong in prison chains. Thereafter he has triumphed most gloriously with the continual favor of successes by the help of the martyr over all his enemies. You know therefore most certainly what kind of love it was, by which once king and martyr loved each other mutually, which neither death nor the sword has abolished: For "love is strong as death"; [Song of Solomon 8:6] and while everything passes away, "love never faileth." [I Corinthians 13:8] This is the beautiful gate, which remained whole and intact in the destruction of Jerusalem; and while all is destroyed in death, love does not perish in death, to whose strength death itself succumbs."

Gerald of Wales

Write a response to each of the following questions;

a) Why is this source valuable to the historian for an enquiry into the Great Rebellion?

Explain your answer using the source, the information given about it and your own knowledge of the historical context.

b) How much weight do you give to the evidence of this source for an enquiry into the guilt of the murder of Thomas Becket?

Explain your answer using the source, the information given about it and your own knowledge of the historical context.

Spend no more than 45 minutes on this question

The Peace of Falaise and the aftermath

By December 1174 almost all opposition to Henry II had been eliminated. The King of France, Henry's wayward sons and the Counts of Blois and Flanders had been reconciled to Henry II. One final problem was overcome in December, when at Falaise in Normandy, William the Lion was brought before Henry and his assembled lords.

William the Lion was released on condition that he became a vassal of Henry II. In effect William the Lion had surrendered the sovereignty of his kingdom in exchange for his release and reinstatement.

In early 1175 Henry and the Young King returned together to England. They now underwent a public tour of the country demonstrating that they were reconciled and urging any final rebels to surrender.

Key rebels such as the Earls of Leicester and Chester were stripped of their lands imprisoned at Salisbury castle. Another inmate of Salisbury castle was Queen Eleanor. She had been supported her sons and encouraged them to rebel. She would now be kept in comfortable house arrest for the remainder of Henry II's reign.

Why did Henry II succeed?

Henry II had acted with decisiveness and aggression throughout the Great Rebellion. He had seen the threat perhaps a little too late and taken by surprise by the reaction of his children at the conference of Limoges in February 1173, but once the threat was realised Henry II had placed his forces on a war footing, alerting his castles so that they had lots of supplies and were adequately protected.

Henry II had also called up large numbers of mercenaries to supplement his military might. He was able to do this because he had ready access through his Wardrobe and Exchequer to large amounts of cash.

Henry II also had a wide basis of support. His Justiciar and sheriffs in England remained loyal even without direct supervision and were able to slow down and blunt the initial force of the rebellion in England and the invasion by the King of Scotland. King Henry II had also retained the wider support of the common people in both England and on the continent. Neither joined the rebellion in any large numbers.

The public act of penance at Canterbury also was of great help to Henry II. The Church saw that Henry II had regretted the death of Thomas Becket. He had publically swore on several occasions that he had no part in the Archbishops' murder, including at Avranches in 1172, but mud has a habit of sticking and suspicion remained. Now even those who had thought Henry II complicit in the murder of Becket were convinced that Henry II truly regretted the murder of the Archbishop and had through his scourging and penance, atoned for this murder.

Becket had already been credited with the performance of miracles that only a saint could do; now Becket would be venerated even more widely and Canterbury would increasingly become a place of pilgrimage.

Task: The Great Rebellion

Write a response to the following question;

The Great Rebellion against Henry II failed primarily through the lack of effective leadership in the opposition. To what extent does the evidence support this view?

Spend no more than 45 minutes on this question

4.3 Henry II and the Papacy

In this section we will;

- *Explore the relationship between Henry II and the various Popes*
- *Understand the significance of the Compromise of Avranches in 1172*
- *Consider the extent to which Henry II's foreign and domestic policies were influenced by the Papacy*
- *Consider the extent to which Henry II was interested in Crusades*

Introduction

In this section we will explore the relationship between the Popes and Henry II.

Papal Relations

There were several Popes during Henry II's reign;

- *Adrian IV (1154-1159)*
- *Alexander III (1159-81)*
- *Lucius III (1181-1185)*
- *Urban III (1185-1187)*
- *Gregory VIII (1187)*
- *Clement III (1187-1191)*

Adrian IV (1154-1159)

Pope Adrian IV was something unique in Papal history. He is to date the only Englishmen ever to be Pope and perhaps his nationality had some influence on the mutual good relations that are evident between Henry II and the Papacy at this time. Both Henry II and Adrian IV came to power at the same time; in 1154 and the pair were soon in communication.

In 1155 Adrian IV issued a papal bull called *'Laudabiliter'*. *Laudabiliter* was an appeal to Henry II to actively take steps to reform the Church in Ireland. In practice this was a permission to invade Ireland and seize control. Henry II on hearing of *Laudabiliter* did not take immediate action. As we have seen, Henry II was far too busy in transforming his newly acquired kingdom of England and in securing his continental possessions to be seriously considering a new adventure in Ireland. However, when Anglo-Norman adventurers such as FitzStephen and Strongbow did begin to conquer Ireland, they did so in part justified by *Laudabiliter*.

In 1156 Henry II communicated with Adrian IV. Henry's father Geoffrey had died with a Will that provided some lands and estates to his other sons; Henry's brothers Geoffrey and William. The result had been a small war between Henry II and Geoffrey over the question of Anjou. Henry II appealed to Pope Adrian IV to have his father's Will set aside and also to release Henry II from the oath that he had sworn to his father to abide by the terms of this Will.

Alexander III (1159-1181)

The Papal election of Alexander III was extraordinary. During his coronation ceremony in Rome, a rival Cardinal, supported by the Emperor Frederick Barbarossa, was a little too eager to claim the Papal throne for himself. As the ceremony progressed, this rival ran into the centre of the service clutching his own Papal robes and regalia and swiftly donning the garments, then ran for the throne of Saint Peter and sat down in it before Alexander III and proclaimed himself Pope Victor IV.

The result was that there were two Popes – the Pope Alexander III and the anti-pope Victor IV. Both Popes struggled for supremacy in Rome and appealed to the rulers of Europe for their support. Victor IV was supported by Frederick Barbarossa; Alexander III was supported by the kings of England, France and Hungary.

In 1162 Alexander III was forced out of Rome and took refuge in France. He would remain an exile for three years until 1165, but be forced out of Rome again in 1167. As a result of being an exile, Alexander III was very much in need of assistance and support from secular rulers friendly to him. Since Alexander III was in France, he consistently supported the policies of Louis VII.

With regards to Henry II, Alexander III was more conflicted. In this period of exile Alexander III could not afford to alienate Henry II and would not have had much reason to do so if not for the Becket controversy. Becket too was an exile and in this Alexander III could sympathise. Alexander III however was somewhat reluctant to

Interdict

An Interdict was a Church ban on individuals and groups, including whole kingdoms, on performing certain church rights that were integral for the cohesion and function of society. The ceremonies banned would usually include mass, baptism, confession and marriage; these had deep impacts on a medieval society.

actively support Becket in his accusations and protestations. In early 1170, the Pope, now back in Rome, encouraged Becket and Henry II to end their disagreements and in part it was through these efforts that Becket was able to return to England.

The murder of Becket at the end of 1170 caused Pope Alexander to heavily censure Henry II. In this he was urged by Louis VII to declare Henry II a murderer and to excommunicate him. Alexander III however seems to have held back from explicitly punishing Henry II. He could have imposed an Interdict on Henry's lands, he could have declared Henry II excommunicate. But he did not.

Instead Alexander III utilised diplomatic pressure on Henry II to repent. He held the threats of interdiction and excommunication as weapons to use on Henry should they be required. Henry II in turn made himself scarce. He went as far as possible away from the public eye and spent several months in Ireland, ostensibly acting on the papal command of *Laudabiliter*, holding Church synods in Ireland whilst ensuring that his Anglo-Norman barons there acknowledged his authority.

What was the Compromise of Avranches?

The Compromise of Avranches in 1172 was a meeting between Henry II and Papal legates designed to bring about reconciliation between Henry II and the Catholic Church.

The need for the Compromise of Avranches

After the murder of Thomas Becket in 1170, relations between the Catholic Church and Henry II deteriorated badly. Although Henry II always denied that he had ordered Becket's murder, the Papacy took a very dim view of anyone that could be seen to be murdering senior clergy. The result was that Henry was vulnerable to a whole raft of punishments that could be meted out by the Catholic Church. Henry could be personally excommunicated; all his lands and subjects could be placed under interdict. The Papacy could encourage rivals like Louis VII to attack Henry II militarily; Henry II's tenants in chief could be encouraged to disobey Henry and even rebel.

In the 1160s the German Emperor Frederick Barbarossa had suffered excommunication for backing a rival pope and over the issues of appointing Bishops in the towns and cities of Germany. The result was a decade or so of trouble for Frederick.

Ironically, Henry II had hoped to profit from some of Frederick's troubles caused by these arguments with the Papacy. In 1166 Henry II had married his eldest daughter Matilda to Frederick Barbarossa's chief tenant in chief and major rival Henry the Lion; Duke of Saxony. Henry II then had no desire to experience the same treatment.

The Compromise of Avranches

On 21 May 1172, at the cathedral of Avranches in Normandy, Henry II met with Papal legates and was publicly acknowledged to have had no part in the murder of Archbishop Thomas Becket. By doing so, Henry II managed to secure again good relations with the papacy.

It was not quite a full pardon. Henry II only secured this acknowledgment from the Papacy on condition that he provided two hundred knights to serve in the Holy Land for a period of one year. Henry himself also swore to go on crusade, either in Palestine or in Spain.

Henry also had to restore all properties that he had seized from the Archbishopric of Canterbury, and also to allow the English church to appeal to Rome in the event of any future disagreement, and to eliminate all customs to which the Church objected. In future the secular courts would have jurisdiction over the clergy, with the exceptions of high treason, highway robbery and arson: the Benefit of Clergy provision in English law. In this respect several of the Constitutions of Clarendon, that Henry II had argued with Becket over so violently, were now rescinded.

Alexander III and Henry II 1173-1181

After the compromise of Avranches, relations between Henry II and Alexander III improved. Alexander III declared Becket a saint in 1173 – an extremely rapid promotion for the Archbishop to Sainthood. Typically the Catholic Church takes decades, even centuries to promote someone to Sainthood. For Becket, the process had taken less than three years. Henry had undergone penance to the newly appointed saint in 1174 during the Great Rebellion and therefore tacitly agreed with the policy put forward by the Pope.

Alexander III continued to work towards reconciliation. In 1177 at Vitry-le-Francois Pope Alexander III organised a reconciliation between Louis VII and Henry II which would last until Louis VII's death in 1180. Alexander also adopted a pragmatic approach to Henry II's promises at Avranches. He never applied much pressure on Henry for him to fulfil his crusading vow.

Task: Henry and Alexander in 1167

The following are excerpts from a Letter of Pope Alexander to Henry, king of England regarding Thomas Becket. In 1167 Alexander III was in exile from Rome.

"The bishop Alexander, servant of the servants of God, to his beloved son, Henry, the illustrious king of the English, health and the Apostolic benediction. With what paternal and kindly feelings we have often convened your royal excellence, and have frequently exhorted you, both by letters and our nuncios, to become reconciled to our venerable brother Thomas, archbishop of Canterbury, and to restore to him and his clerks their churches, with the other things which you have taken from them, the prudence of your highness is by no means unaware, inasmuch as it is public and notorious to nearly the whole of Christendom. Wherefore, seeing that we have hitherto been able to make but little progress in this matter, or by kind and gentle conduct to soothe the emotions of your mind, we are rendered sad and sorrowful, and grieve that we are disappointed in our hopes and expectations; particularly as we love you sincerely as our most dearly-beloved son in the Lord, and we see this great danger threatening you...We have determined no longer to bear your hardness of heart as heretofore, to the detriment of justice and your own salvation; nor will we for the future close the mouth of the said archbishop in any way, or prevent him from freely doing his duty, and avenging with the sword of ecclesiastical severity the wrongs which have been done to himself and to the Church entrusted to his charge...."

Write a response to the following question;

a) Why is this source valuable to the historian for an enquiry into Henry's relationship with the Papacy?

Explain your answer using the source, the information given about it and your own knowledge of the historical context.

b) How much weight do you give to the evidence of this source for an enquiry into the power of the Church in 12th century politics?

Explain your answer using the source, the information given about it and your own knowledge of the historical context.

Spend no more than 45 minutes on this question

Task: Henry and Alexander in 1169

The following are excerpts of a Letter of Pope Alexander III to Henry, king of England in 1169

"the letter which your excellency transmitted...we have received with the more kindly feelings, and have with the greater favour and honour granted the prayer thereof... the more that in our greatest necessity we have experienced your most devoted sincerity towards us. For our memory at no time hereafter will be able possibly to lose the recollection of the marks of duty shown to us by you at a time so opportune, nor will they by any lapse of time be overshadowed in the sight of the church...being not unmindful however, as we have already mentioned, of your praiseworthy and distinguished dutifulness to us. These we have thought fit to send to the presence of your highness, with full powers to take cognizance of and give judgment upon the ecclesiastical matters which are the subject of dispute between you and our venerable brother, the archbishop of Canterbury, ...with regard to the appeal made unto ourselves, and such other matters in dispute in your kingdom as they shall be enabled to bring to a satisfactory conclusion, and, according as the Lord shall give them His assistance therein, to terminate the same in a canonical manner. We shall by all means also forbid the said archbishop in any way to attempt to molest, or disturb, or disquiet either yourself, or your people, or the kingdom entrusted to your government, until these matters in dispute shall have been brought to a legitimate conclusion. But, if the aforesaid archbishop shall in the meantime, pronounce any sentence upon you, or your kingdom, or any person in your realm, we do pronounce the same to be null and void, and not in any way to affect you. To put an end to such a course, and as a proof of our wishes, you are, in case necessity shall arise for so doing, to produce this present letter. But, otherwise, we do beg of your serene highness, and strongly recommend you, not to let this letter or the tenor thereof be known to any person whatsoever, but to keep it entirely secret. And as for those persons of your household and your advisers, whom the said archbishop has already subjected to sentence of excommunication, the parties sent by us will, with the Lord's assistance, absolve them. Put if, in the meantime, any one of them shall be in fear of immediate death, we do grant that he may be absolved by any bishop, or religious and discreet man, on the oath being administered to him, according to the custom of the Church, that if he shall recover he will consider himself bound to obey our mandates."

Write a response to the following question;

a) Why is this source valuable to the historian for an enquiry into Henry's relationship with the Papacy? Explain your answer using the source, the information given about it and your own knowledge of the historical context.

b) How much weight do you give to the evidence of this source for an enquiry into the power of the Church in 12th century diplomacy? Explain your answer using the source, the information given about it and your own knowledge of the historical context.

Spend no more than 45 minutes on this question

Henry II and the Popes 1181-1189

After the death of Pope Alexander III in 1181 relations with the papacy became increasingly concerned with trying to get Henry II to use his power and authority for the benefit of the crusader states.

Henry II had sworn to go on Crusade at Avranches in 1172, but so far he had done little to help his co-religionists in Palestine and Syria. After the death of the leper king Baldwin IV in 1185 Henry II had refused an appeal by the Patriarch of Jerusalem to travel to Palestine and to take up the kingship. This was not as outlandish an appeal as it first seems, Henry II's grandfather Fulk, Count of Anjou had gone to Jerusalem to become King.

Henry II and the Third Crusade

In October 1187 Jerusalem was captured by Saladin, the bad news travelled swiftly and may have hastened the death of Pope Urban III. The newly appointed Pope Gregory VIII called for a new crusade in his papal bull *'Audita Tremendi'*. In November 1187, Richard swore to take the cross and join the crusade. Such a hasty move further alienated Henry II from his son as he was somewhat more reluctant to partake in the crusade.

In January 1188 the Archbishop Josias met the Kings of Henry II and Philip Augustus at the town of Gisors on the border of the duchy of Normandy. At Gisors the two kings agreed to a truce and both determined to pledge themselves to the Third Crusade. Joining the kings at Gisors was also Philip, the Count of Flanders. It was decided that all the forces of England, France and Flanders would travel together to Jerusalem. The followers of the English King would wear White Crosses, the French would wear Red Crosses and the followers of the Count of Flanders would wear Green crosses.

Henry II was also somewhat reluctant to go Crusading. He had previously resented attempts to recruit men and money to be as he saw, wasted in Outremer and this reluctance was not helped by Henry's age and state of health. Henry was already ill when he agreed to go on Crusade at Gisors in January 1188. His health was not helped by his son's rebellion and Henry was only able to make a peace with Richard and Philip a few days before his death. Henry had however prepared some of the ground for his successor; permitting the raising of the Saladin Tithe, and preparing the fleet in England, which sailed under the Archbishop of Canterbury.

The Saladin Tithe

It was also decided at Gisors to arrange and regulate taxes that would finance the Crusade expeditions. The Saladin Tithe was a 10% flat rate tax on income and moveable property of all subjects of the kings. Only those that were to go on the Crusade expedition were to be exempt and therefore the application of this tax was a great encouragement to many to join the crusade; particularly the wealthy and those who could afford to best fight as knights. Many peasants had little disposal income and less moveable property that could be taxed. Lords and knights on the other hand had more coin, more luxurious goods and livestock, and so faced a large tax bill. The Saladin Tithe could be avoided if an individual went and joined the Crusade.

The lands of the English king were better organised and regulated and the Saladin Tithe was rigidly enforced most effectively by King Henry and subsequently by his son and heir Richard. However, King William of Scotland, who was subject to King Henry and therefore the Saladin Tithe, was unable to compel his lords to participate in raising the Saladin Tithe.

Henry also had to face some abuse of this extraordinary tax. A Templar knight, called Gilbert of Hoxton, tried to steal the Saladin Tithe that he was entrusted with.

Dissent and delay

The meeting at Gisors promised an emphatic Crusade response from the rulers of England and France; however this Crusade response faced delays and procrastinations as it became clear that the Papal truce was less important than the immediate squabbles of the lords of the land.

Henry's heir, Richard faced a revolt in his lands in Aquitaine in June 1188 and in addition he could not halt a border war with his neighbour and rival the Count of Toulouse. Despite his family's record in Crusading history, the current Count of Toulouse had little interest in heading to Jerusalem and was happy to ignore the Papal Truce of 1187. The border war escalated and King Philip of France decided to intervene and invaded Richard's lands. King Henry II in turn began to attack King Philip's land in Northern France. By January 1189 this war took on a new twist when Richard rebelled against his father and joined the French king in attacks on Henry's lands in Normandy, Maine and Anjou. Peace was not restored until the 3rd of July 1189 and only three days later, King Henry of England himself died, leaving Richard King of England.

Task: Henry II the Crusader

Write a response to the following question;

Henry II had absolutely no interest in joining or supporting any Crusading endeavour. To what extent do you agree with this view?

Spend no more than 45 minutes on this question

4.4 Henry II and the extension of Royal Authority 1175-1182

In this section we will;

- *Explore the years 1175-1182*
- *Explore the later legal reforms of Henry II*
- *Consider the challenges that came from Henry II's family in this period*
- *Explore the relationship between Henry II and Louis VII*

Introduction

Henry II had faced down the major crisis of the Great Rebellion and everywhere he seemed triumphant. His enemies and rivals had been defeated militarily and brought to accept peace. His rebellious earls and barons had been captured, killed or brought to heel, and his rebellious sons made aware that here and now, they were no match for the old king.

Henry exerts his authority

At Falaise in1174, Henry released the captured King of Scotland, William the Lion. In return, William the Lion had to swear homage to Henry II and his heirs as his overlord for the possession of Scotland.

Henry II and the Young King then conducted a joint tour of England. This tour was a clear demonstration that the pair were reconciled and that Henry had forgiven his wayward son. For his part, Henry the Young King would begin to serve more diligently as his father's lieutenant. Henry was determined to exert his authority over the English barons. He ordered the surrender of all castles to himself and his own representatives. Some castles were deemed illegal and destroyed, others were returned to their previous owners and others were retained by the King and garrisoned with his own men and sheriffs that he appointed.

Other castles were rebuilt and refortified using the wealth of Henry II to make them more impressive and secure. The Tower of London underwent improvements as did Windsor castle, Newcastle Upon Tyne and Winchester but the most significant demonstration of this was at Dover castle. This showpiece castle was designed to impress visitors from the continent coming into England via Dover but also to provide a serious barrier to any potential invasion force. In all

Henry II would spend some £21000 on castle building during his reign.

In 1175 Henry II presided over the Treaty of Windsor, a settled agreement for the partition of the island of Ireland between those areas ruled by the Anglo-Normans and those regions governed by the Kings of Ireland. Henry's youngest son, John now aged eight, was appointed 'lord of Ireland'. This agreement provisioned Henry's youngest son with lands and title that crucially did not impinge on those regions and titles already allocated to his other sons.

Judicial and governmental reform

In 1176 Henry had ordered some reforms of the judicial system of England. The Assize of Northampton was the result and these reforms that reissued and strengthened some of the provisions of the Assize of Clarendon, were further followed with by new laws and procedures.

The Assize of Northampton

In 1176, England had recently suffered another period of civil war. Henry II had taken steps to eliminate the causes and grievances of those that had joined the rebellion against him and the Assize of Northampton was one of these steps to amend the harshness and possible sources of abuse that had resulted from the Assize of Clarendon.

The Assize of Northampton was a series of commands agreed upon by King Henry II of England and his major tenants in chief in council at Northampton in 1176. The Assize of Northampton was issued as instructions to establish six committees of three judges each. Each committee being responsible for one of six divisions of England, called circuits. These judicial committees would visit these circuits and oversee judicial affairs within this circuit. Much of assize of Northampton contains instructions to judges that concern their various administrative, political, judicial, and financial duties.

Some parts of the Assize of Northampton repeated some of the provisions of the Assize of Clarendon of 1166, but there were several differences. The second part of the assize defined some of the rights of heirs, the rights of lords and widows of a deceased free tenant; known as *mort d'ancestor*. In line with *mort d'ancestor*, the justices were also ordered to hear pleas of *novel disseisin*, which was an action to recover lands of which the complainant had been dispossessed in cases that had arisen arising since May 1175 and also to scrutinise actions commenced by the king's orders for the recovery of land which was held by the service of half a knight's fee or less.

These procedures include the reorganisation of the Curia Regis in 1178, whereby five delegated members of the Curia Regis would remain permanently stationed at Westminster as a permanent court called 'the court of the king's bench' or what would become the origins of the supreme court in England.

Further judicial reforms included in the assize of Northampton were the so called 'petty assizes' of *Mort d'ancestor, Darrein presentment* and *novel disseisin;*

The petty assizes

The assize of mort d'ancestor, novel disseisin, darrein presentment was one of the so-called petty assizes established by the Assize of Clarendon in 1166. These were minor regulations contained within the greater umbrella of the Assizes of Clarendon in 1166 and the subsequent Assize of Northampton in 1177.

- ***mort d'ancestor***

mort d'ancestor or 'death of ancestor') was an action brought where a complainant claimed that the defendant had entered upon a freehold belonging to themselves following the death of one of his relatives.

- ***darrein presentment***

The darrein presentment was a legal action was related to the privilege of a landowner, often associated with a fee, of the right to appoint a caretaker or parson to a particular parish. Darrein presentment (also known as "last presentation") was a legal decision to conduct an inquiry into who in fact was the last patron to present a donation to a church then vacant, of which the plaintiff had complained that he was unlawfully deprived by the defendant.

- ***novel disseisin***

novel disseisin or 'recent dispossession' was an action to recover lands of which the complainant had been dispossessed (disseised). This action became extremely popular due mostly to its rapid process. novel disseisin simply required the complainant to request an inquiry over whether a dispossession had actually taken place. If it had, the property was restored and the question of true ownership was dealt with later.

In 1181 the Assize of Arms was issued. This Assize arranged the reorganisation and tightening up of payments of scutage.

Diplomacy

On the diplomatic front, Henry also spread his authority with some success. The kings of Navarre and Castile appealed to Henry II to resolve their differences which he successfully did. In 1176 Henry II married his daughter Joan to William II of Sicily; a young, energetic and vibrant kingdom in the centre of the Mediterranean. The next year, in 1177 Henry arranged the marriage of his daughter Eleanor to Alfonso of Castile. The same year Louis VII and Henry II met at Ivry in a meeting arranged by Pope Alexander III. The two monarchs arranged a treaty of non-aggression and to;

"henceforth to be friends, and that each of us will to take best of his ability defend the other in life and limb".

Henry II did however resist urgent appeals by Cardinal Huguzon, the Papal legate, to go on Crusade to Palestine. In 1179, King Louis VII, feeling perhaps the series of illnesses that would contribute to his death requested of Henry II that he be allowed to undertake a pilgrimage to the shrine of Thomas Becket at Canterbury. Henry II agreed and the pilgrimage undertook some of the hallmarks of a state visit, with Henry II eager to show off his magnificent new castle at Dover.

Henry the Young King during the years 1175-1181

Henry the Young King had been chastised by his defeat in the Great Rebellion of 1173-1174. Henry's grievance that he had no lands to rule was countered by Henry II by the granting of a massive allowance of some £15000 annually for his to keep and maintain his own court and retinue. This money and wealth allowed the Young King to present himself around continental Europe at the many tournaments that were popular amongst the knights and lords of France.

After a less than auspicious start, that involved the Young King and his men being seen as the whipping boys of many a tournament, the Young King and his retinue started to achieve a measure of respectability at these events. The Young king's brother Geoffrey was also a keen tournament participant; but less fortunate – he would be killed as a result of injuries sustained in a tournament in 1186.

The Young King was also used by Henry II as his chief lieutenant in the years 1175-1180. He represented the king at court in the absence of his father. In 1176-1177 the Young King was sent to the Duchy of Aquitaine to deal with rebellion. In 1180 the Young King also led his father's forces against raiding parties of knights from Flanders and Burgundy.

Louis VII died in 1180, but in the year before his son had been crowned as *rex designatus* in 1179. Henry the Young King was sent to take part in this ceremony held at Rheims. Henry's entourage was grander than that led by Thomas Becket, with the Young King being accompanied by no fewer than five hundred knights.

Task: Henry II in the years 1175-1182

Write a response to the following question;

Henry II acts in the years 1175-1182 were primarily part of a continuing policy to obtain more money. To what extent do you agree with this view?

Spend no more than 45 minutes on this question

Louis VII

Louis VII was king of France from 1137-1180 and was Henry II's long-time rival and sparring partner. The French king was famed for his piety and austere behaviour and Louis was perhaps most famous for his participation in the Second Crusade.

In many ways the Second Crusade was illuminating of the king's character, individually brave, pious and intelligent, Louis VII lacked the military strategic vision to be a great general and whilst mostly diplomatically astute, lacked the moral authority to exert his will over his peers and tenants-in-chief. A case in point was Louis VII's relations with Henry II. Louis VII just did not really know how to treat with Henry II. As king of England, Henry II was in many ways Louis' equal, as Duke of Normandy, Henry was Louis VII's vassal and a tenant in chief.

Louis VII also viewed Henry II with suspicion when it came to his ambition; when the Duke of Brittany Conrad was faced with rebellion in his own lands, technically it should have been Louis VII to whom he appealed for assistance. However, Henry II was closer, his lands neighboured Brittany and Henry had also married his son Geoffrey to Conrad's daughter. Louis VII then was disgruntled that Henry II took advantage of the situation to arrange matters in Brittany as he saw fit.

Louis VII had limited options in his dealings with Henry II. He could protest (but was often ignored), he could annoy or injury him diplomatically were possible (such as when harboured Becket) or he could make war on Henry II. Louis VII tried all three options with varying levels of success. Militarily, Louis VII's many wars with Henry II had mixed levels of failure.

Wars between Henry II and Louis VII occurred in the following years;

- 1155
- 1157
- 1159
- 1166-1169
- 1173-1174

Most of these wars consisted of low level raids and sieges of castles and towns. For the most part these wars were begun by Louis VII, either by himself or with allies such as Philip of Flanders and Henry's own sons. Ironically it was Henry II's own sons proved to be Louis VII's most useful allies in the wars against Henry II.

Louis VII had better success on the diplomatic front against Henry II. By sheltering Becket, siding with the Count of Toulouse in 1159 and by encouraging Henry's own sons to resent their father and even rebel in 1173-4, but even in combination with the Great Rebellion of 1173-1174, Louis VII lacked the military will and resources to really take the battle to Henry II.

Louis VII's family and marriages

Louis VII had come to the kingship of France at an early age as *rex designatus* in 1131, aged eleven. In 1137, aged seventeen, Louis VII became king in his own right when his father Louis VI died.

Louis VII was married three times;

- Eleanor of Aquitaine from 1137-1152 when the marriage was annulled.
- Constanza of Castile from 1154-1160 when Constanza died in childbirth.
- Adele of Champagne from 1160 until Louis' death in 1180.

Louis VII had several children;

- Marie and Alix by Eleanor of Aquitaine
- Margaret and Alice by Constanza of Castile
- Philip Augustus by Adele of Champagne in 1165

Much of Louis VII's concern in his marriages was the lack of a male heir. As a result, before 1165, Louis VII had to seek suitable husbands for his daughters, who could if necessary inherit the Kingdom of France. Again however, the spectre of Henry II loomed over this policy. The two eldest daughters of Louis VII were his children with Eleanor, now Queen of England. The next pair of daughters, Margaret and Alice, from his marriage with Constanza of Castile, were given up to Henry II as diplomatic trophies. Margaret married Henry the Young King and Alice was betrothed at an early age to Richard. These planned marriages provided diplomatic links that could strengthen relations between the two monarchs, however, if Louis VII continued to lack a male heir, Henry the Young King had through his marriage to Margaret, a link to the crown of France itself.

This potential problem went away in 1165 after the birth of Philip Augustus, but Henry II continued to hold Alice as a potential hostage, denying his son Richard the planned marriage to Alice and even according to rumour, seducing the girl himself. If this was the case the aim could only have been to embarrass Louis VII by his impotence to prevent such a situation.

Louis and Henry II 1174-1180

After the Great Rebellion, both rulers seem to have made more effort to improve their relationship. At the urging of Pope Alexander III the two kings were formerly reconciled in 1177 and in 1178 Louis VII requested permission of Henry II to undertake a pilgrimage to visit the tomb of Becket at Canterbury. Henry II gladly agreed, but used the occasion to showcase his new castle at Dover; a clear demonstration of Henry's wealth and military might.

Shortly after the pilgrimage Louis VII arranged to have his son Philip Augustus crowned *rex designatus* in 1179, but took ill and in a long period of illness Louis VII was incapable of effective governorship. On the 18th September 1180, he died.

Henry's Will

In February 1182 Henry II, now aged forty nine years of age, wrote his Will to formerly divide his inheritance amongst his sons;

- Henry the Young King would be Count of Anjou, Duke of Normandy and King of England
- Richard would be Count of Poitiers and Duke of Aquitaine
- Geoffrey would be Duke of Brittany
- John would be King of Ireland

In many ways this will simply reconfirmed the Conference of Montmirail of 1169 – and like the Conference of Montmirail, the creation of this Will and the confirmation of his sons' inheritance, led to trouble.

Henry the Young King had acted as his father's loyal lieutenant since the Great Rebellion. He was *rex designatus*, he had represented him on embassies, he had led military expeditions against rebel lords and he had acquired a name for himself on the tournament fields of

Western Europe. He was however now twenty seven years of age and he still had no lands to rule.

The Young King demanded of his father that he be granted either the County of Anjou, the Duchy of Normandy or the Kingdom of England for him to rule. This he declared would give him land equal to his status and make him equal to his brothers in having lands to rule. Henry II refused.

It was almost a repetition of the arguments at Limoges of 1172, like before; Henry II offered his son no lands. Instead; he offered him more money. The Young King went to Paris and there pledged to go on a pilgrimage to the Holy Land.

Alienation at Le Mans

In January 1183 Henry II summoned his sons to a great conference at Le Mans. Also present was his daughter Matilda and her husband Henry the Lion of Saxony. The conference was a grand affair, with feasting and hunting and over one thousand knights being present. Henry II hoped for reconciliation with his son and heir. Henry desired to satisfy his eldest son; not with land but with authority over his brothers. To this end Henry II declared that Richard and Geoffrey would give homage to the Young King for their lands.

There were several problems with this approach. First of all, it did not give the Young King what he desired; lands of his own. Secondly, the Young King had no legal right to receive this homage – Richard and Geoffrey had already given their homage to another for the possession of their respective lands; the King of France. Thirdly, such a move would anger the French King Philip Augustus.

The result was a spectacular fall out. Geoffrey duly gave his homage for Brittany to the Young King. Richard however refused outright and left the conference to prepare his lands and supporters for war.

Henry the Young King pledged his loyalty to his father but sent messengers to sympathetic lords in Aquitaine and encouraged them to rebel against Richard. Geoffrey swore to support the Young King in any confrontation with Richard and perhaps the Young King, who had good relations with the French King Philip Augustus, perhaps had his support also. The Young King perhaps hoped that given Richard's refusal to pledge his allegiance to himself, he would be able to take control of the Duchy of Aquitaine for himself.

The death of the Young King

In February 1183, a mercenary army paid for by the Young King attacked Aquitaine. They were heavily defeated in battle by Richard who demonstrated some of the tactical ability that would stand him in good stead in Palestine in a decades' time.

In March 1183 the Young King began to raid Aquitainian regions and succeeded with the help of Geoffrey and rebel lords to occupy the region of Limoges. However, Richard defended his lands well and retaliated with raids of his own. Henry II watched his sons wage war on each other for a few weeks and then made his decision. He would support Richard.

Once Henry II had made this decision, diplomatic pressure on the Young King and Geoffrey was brought to bear. The Young King was declared excommunicated by the Pope and Geoffrey pressured to surrender by attacks on Brittany. Henry II also arranged to meet Geoffrey at Limoges whose men, by accident or design, attempted to assassinate Henry II himself on two occasions. Chastened, Geoffrey agreed to cease his attacks on Richard and returned to Brittany. Henry the Young King however continued with his attacks on Richard, making little headway. Then in early June the Young King took ill of dysentery and on the 11th June 1183 he died.

The Young King had remained Henry II's heir despite his numerous rebellions. He had demonstrated his eagerness for land consistently and perhaps if his father had granted him a region like Anjou he may have satisfied his son's ambitions in that regard. However, given that the Young King had rebelled on several occasions, perhaps Henry II was justified in denying his son lands. After all, he may have then wanted more.

> ***Task: Henry and his sons***
>
> *Henry's troubles with his sons were largely of his own making. To what extent do you agree with this view?*
>
> ***Spend no more than 30 minutes on this question***

4.5 Henry II: the final years 1185-1189

In this section we will;

- *Explore the years 1185-1189*
- *Explore the challenges faced by Henry II in the years 1185-1189*
- *Consider the challenges that came from Henry II's family in this period*
- *Explore the relationship between Henry II and Philip Augustus*

Introduction

In the years 1185-1189 we now reach the final years of the life of Henry II. So far, Henry II had been able to deal with whatever challenge had been presented to him. However, he now faced two men who had seen how Henry II had ruled and dominated his rivals. These men would now use these lessons against Henry II himself. One was the king of France, Philip Augustus; the other was Richard, Henry's son and heir.

Philip II Augustus

Philip II of France, often nicknamed Augustus, was crowned *rex designatus* in 1179, aged fourteen, when it became clear that Louis VII health was in terminal decline. He would rule as the King of France until his death in 1223. Philip II acquired his nickname 'Augustus' from a French monk who described him as such because he extended the power and authority of the French crown.

In some ways Philip Augustus' kingship was influenced by Henry II. He had seen that Henry II had acquired lands, territory and authority through force of personality, energy and diplomatic astuteness. Philip Augustus II career and successes too could be attributed to the template established by his father's rival Henry II.

The increasing authority of the French crown 1180-1189

Philip Augustus was fifteen when he became sole ruler of France in 1180. He was soon making his presence felt; he engaged in a war with Philip of Flanders, but it came clear during this war that the French crown lacked the deep financial resources of his Angevin rival to really make his authority felt. In 1181 then, to address this shortfall, Philip Augustus took the decision to expel the Jewish population from his towns and lands and in doing so seized their wealth.

In 1183 with the death of Henry the Young King, Philip Augustus saw another opportunity to acquire wealth and land. Henry's wife Margaret was Philip's half-sister and childless. He therefore insisted that her dowry, the region of the Vexin, be returned to the French crown to be reissued in the future as Margaret's dowry when she should marry another husband. Henry II at first refused to agree with this move, but Margaret was soon betrothed to the new king of Hungary; like the French crown, a staunch ally of the Papacy. Once this marriage was arranged Henry II had no choice but to agree.

In 1185 another opportunity for Philip Augustus to exert his authority was at the Treaty of Boves. With this treaty the war with Philip, Count of Flanders was resolved and the price of this peace with the Count of Flanders was the acquisition of some lands in Flanders for the French crown.

In 1186, Henry II's son Geoffrey was killed in a tournament melee. He was Duke of Brittany and since the conference of Montmirail, the Duke of Brittany had given homage to the French crown. Like Henry the Young King he died without an heir (his wife was pregnant with a son who would be born months later; of course at the time of Geoffrey's death the fate of this child was anything but certain.) Philip Augustus therefore demanded that the Duchy be restored to the French crown.

Henry II refused but was technically standing on very slippery ground, a war between Henry II and Philip Augustus resulted from 1186-1188 only ended by the peace ordered by the Pope after the capture of Jerusalem, but to subsequently flare up again until the death of King Henry II.

Task: Henry and Philip Augustus

To what extent do you agree with the view that Philip Augustus followed the example of Henry II more than the example of his own father Louis VII?

Spend no more than 45 minutes on this question

The alienation of Richard

With the death of the Young King, Henry II now had to rethink the distribution of his inheritance and his lands now began to diminish. Philip Augustus demanded and in time received the Vexin back from Henry II; this region had been granted as Margaret's dowry when she married Young Henry.

Henry II also now had a new heir as it would be Richard who was to succeed him. In many ways this was advantageous. Richard had consistently demonstrated that he was the most able of his sons and had demonstrated that he was the most like his father in political astuteness. It would be Richard who would inherit Anjou, Normandy and England when Henry II died.

Here though was a new problem. Richard was already Count of Poitiers and Duke of Aquitaine. If he retained these lands he would possess much more potential power and authority than Henry II had envisaged for the Young King.

By the autumn of 1183, the solution then as Henry II saw it was for Richard to surrender Aquitaine – not to Geoffrey who still possessed Brittany, and had demonstrated his character by his willingness to permit his men to try and kill Henry II himself, but rather to John. Richard however had other views. He refused to surrender Aquitaine; a region he had governed since he was a child and indeed grown up in.

Henry II had only limited options regarding Richard. He could continue to encourage him to do what the saw was the right thing; to surrender Aquitaine and in turn assume the position previously occupied by the Young King, he could force him by the threat of or an actual invasion of Aquitaine; an expensive proposition that would only serve to make both father and son poorer or he could make other arrangements.

It was this third option that Henry II took first. In 1184 Henry gave up trying to coerce Richard to surrender Aquitaine and instead appoint Geoffrey as the son that would inherit Anjou, Normandy and England. John was sent to Ireland to take up his position as King of Ireland.

Richard reacted to this news with an immediate invasion of Brittany. Geoffrey appealed to his father for help and demanded that Anjou be surrendered to him immediately so that he had the resources to fight his brother. Henry II refused and as a result of this fallout Geoffrey left Brittany and went into exile at Paris. He remained at the court of Philip Augustus feasting and hunting with his friend the French king until in 1186 he was killed during a tournament.

Whilst Richard was attacking Brittany, Henry II arrived at a fourth solution. Summoning Queen Eleanor from her house arrest in England, Henry II demanded that Richard surrender the Duchy of Aquitaine to his mother, through which all of their claims to the Duchy were based. The Aquitainian lords also joined this appeal and Richard grudgingly agreed to surrender the Duchy. He did however remain as Count of Poitiers. For two years, between 1184 and 1186 there was peace between Henry II and his sons.

Philip Augustus' grievances against Henry II

By early 1187 Henry II might have had peace with his sons Richard and John, but a new external threat was emerging. Philip Augustus had been King of France since 1180 and now, aged twenty two, was just beginning to enter full adulthood.

Philip Augustus had already exerted his authority over the Count of Flanders and the other Counts of his kingdom; he had also several reasons to oppose Henry II. These were;

- *The reluctance of Henry II to return the Vexin*
- *The refusal of Henry II to permit Richard and Alice to marry*
- *The position of the Duchy of Brittany after the death of Geoffrey*
- *Border disputes in Berry and Toulouse*

On the death of Henry the Young King in 1183, he had to insist that the dowry granted to Margaret be returned. This dowry, the region of the Vexin, had proved to prise out of Henry's grasp, with the older king only agreeing to do so when Margaret married the King of Hungary, who also had very good relations with the Pope who could also exert his own particular brand of coercion.

A second grievance was the treatment of Alice; Philip Augustus' half-sister. For over a decade Alice had remained in the care of Henry II as the promised wife of Richard. However the marriage had never gone ahead. Politically this oversight might have been overlooked whilst Margaret was married to the Young King, but with the death of the latter in 1183, the French King was aware that he had no outright marriage alliance with Henry II. What was worse, rumours abounded that Henry had seduced Alice himself, treating the young woman more like a courtesan than a princess.

Thirdly, in 1186 on the death of Geoffrey, the Duchy of Brittany had no Duke. Henry II supported the claims of Arthur; Geoffrey's posthumous son, but in 1187 less than a year old. In the meantime of course Henry II would rule Brittany directly himself. Philip disagreed. Geoffrey had ruled Brittany as a tenant-in-chief of the French crown, for which he had sworn homage in 1169 and in 1180. By rights then Philip argued, the duchy should revert back to the French crown. Part of the problem of Philip's position however was that he only had access to Brittany by sea, isolated as it was on the other side of Normandy and Anjou; both possessed by Henry II.

A final grievance of Philip was that his allies in the region of Toulouse and Berry were involved in a border war with Richard, now Count of Poitiers, but eager to assert his authority beyond his own boundaries. The Count of Toulouse appealed to King Philip in late 1186 for assistance against Richard.

Task: Philip Augustus' grievances

Of the four grievances Philip Augustus had with Henry II. Rank these grievances in order of importance. Which do you think was the most and least justified? Explain your reasoning.

Spend no more than 30 minutes on this question

War and the call of the Cross

In 1187 Philip Augustus began to militarily assist the Count of Toulouse against Richard of Poitiers. In person Philip led an attack against Berry and Richard appealed for help from his father. Much of 1187 was spent in a tit-for-tat exchange of raids and counter raids across the Aquitaine-Toulouse border and along the Berry-Maine border.

This war was called to a halt by the declaration of Pope Gregory VIII by the issuing of the Papal Bull *'Audita Tremendi'* commanding all wars in Europe to cease in preparation for a new struggle for a higher cause. In October 1187 Jerusalem had been captured by Saladin and a new Crusade was called to recover the Holy city. In November 1187 Richard took the Cross without consulting his father or asking his permission.

The two kings were placed in an awkward position by *'Audita Tremendi'* with conflicting desires and pressures. Neither King was overly keen to go on crusade; however the loss of Jerusalem was such a major blow to the prestige of Christendom that both rulers were under great pressure to take the Cross. It was clear that both would have to go. If one refused, the other too could not go for fear of losing their lands at home whilst they fought the Crusade. However if they refused to go they risked extreme levels of pressure from their subjects and from the Church. Pragmatically, then an agreement had to be struck and peace restored.

At Gisors in January 1188 both Kings met at a public ceremony of reconciliation and both took the cross, promising to go on Crusade.

Philip Augustus and his motives to join the Third Crusade

According to Steven Runciman, King Philip's motives for going on Crusade went beyond that of considered Christian duty;

> *"...he was no idealist, and he went crusading merely from political necessity."*

Runciman 1954, p34

In 1187, King Philip of France was in his mid-twenties, but had already been King of France for some ten years. His views of Crusading may well have been influenced by the views of his Father on the matter. Louis VII had led the Second Crusade to the fiasco outside Damascus. Despite the piety of Louis VII, that one experience was enough Crusading for him.

However, King Philip needed to go on Crusade because he had been struggling to assert his authority as king. He had been in a series of wars with his rival Henry II, who in addition to being King of England, was also overlord of more territory of France than King Philip himself. King Philip was badly in need of the goodwill of the Church and needed a way to ensure tighter control of the powerful Counts and Dukes of France. King Philip also faced a dilemma; if the English king was to go on Crusade and Philip did not, then those French lords that were going on Crusade would likely fall under the influence of the English King. Likewise, if King Philip went on Crusade and the English King did not, then he risked being unable to defend his lands from any attempt to dispossess him.

The solution therefore required both rulers to go on Crusade.

War between Father and Son

For the first six months of 1188 it seemed that the Crusade preparations were proceeding smoothly. Great lords such as Count Philip of Flanders joined the Crusade, as had many knights and lords. Armies were already sailing out to Palestine, including one led by the Archbishop of Canterbury; extensive funds were being raised through donations and measures such as the 'Saladin tithe'.

However, all was not well and the peace ordered by the Pope did not last. In June 1188 a new border war erupted between Richard and the Count of Toulouse, who despite his family's illustrious crusading pedigree had not taken the cross and was soon joined by new fighting between King Henry II and King Philip Augustus in Berry and Maine. In August 1188 Henry II led an invasion of French lands in person before Papal legates coerced both sides back to the negotiation table.

At Bonmoulins in November 1188 all sides met to try and agree to a ceasefire, however the conference was ended by Richard who requested that his father agree to swear an oath that guaranteed him as Henry II's heir. Such a guarantee on one hand might have been sensible. Richard was Henry's eldest son and the only alternative was John, a much younger and much less experienced man, now just twenty one. However both Henry II and Richard had sworn to go on crusade and this dangerous expedition might well end in death for one or both of them. If both died then John would be the sole surviving heir. In any event both would be absent for several years. In such an event it might be unwise to guarantee Richard the kingship.

Philip Augustus observed this argument and sided with Richard. He requested that Alice marry Richard and received the homage of Richard for Aquitaine in a clear breach with Henry II. Henry II was now losing control. He was less energetic than he was in his youth and already sick with the illness that would kill him within the year. Whilst Philip Augustus and Richard attacked Henry in Aquitaine and Maine, a rebellion erupted in Brittany no doubt encouraged by supporters of the French king.

War continued through the winter of 1188-1189. Maine and Tourraine were attacked and bore the brunt of the fighting. A peace conference in early June 1189 brokered by Papal legates at the castle of La Ferte-Bernard ended inconclusively and this same castle was immediately captured by Philip and Richard after the conference broke up.

Momentum was now firmly with Richard and Philip. On the 12th June, the important town of Le Mans was captured and burned by their forces. Henry II, present in Le Mans, barely escaped; however Richard himself was nearly killed in the same battle. Pursuing his father too eagerly, he was unarmoured when confronted by a knight in the service of Henry II, William Marshall who could have killed him there and then. Instead, William Marshall speared Richard's horse and spared the man. Richard never forgot this and viewed Marshall as a trusted and honourable man thereafter.

Henry II retreated to Chinon castle, very sick and dying. He took to his bed for several weeks. In the meantime the County of Maine was overrun and the town of Tours captured.

On the 3rd of July 1189 a new meeting was arranged between the kings of England and France, with Richard looking on as an observer. Philip Augustus would agree to peace if a whole raft of concessions were agreed to; including payment of a huge sum of money and surrender of land and castles as well as recognizing Richard as his heir. Henry II agreed. Three days later on the 6th July 1189, Henry II died.

Insult to injury

Henry II died shortly after having received a list of names of those people that had betrayed him. One of the first names on this list was his son John. At hearing the name of his son, who he had previously believed loyal, Henry II ordered the man reading the list to stop.

More insult followed. Henry II expired on the 6th July and he was supposed to lay in state. Instead, his servants robbed his body of clothes and jewels, and had his chambers ransacked for money. His body was left lying half out of bed and partially on the floor. A few loyal men, including William Marshall, tended the body with better care and escorted his corpse to Fontevraud Abbey near Chinon.

Task: Henry II and Richard

To what extent do you think Henry II underestimated Richard in the years 1183-1189?

Spend no more than 30 minutes on this question

Henry II: Successes and failures

Henry II was fifty six when he died at Chinon. He had reigned as king of England for almost thirty five years. Henry II established a dynasty, what many would call the Plantagenets; that would rule England for over two hundred years.

Dan Jones (2012, p108) sums up Henry II's life and career as follows;

"Henry's astonishing, incessantly busy life ended in misery. He had been betrayed by his wife and every one of his sons, seen his birthplace reduced to smouldering rubble and suffered humiliation... But he had left his indelible stamp on all of the innumerable places that he had travelled across greater France and the British isles. Until his last years he had mastered every king, duke and count who tested him".

Henry II was certainly ambitious and hardworking. In the sphere of diplomacy he was largely successful. He usually had good relations with the Papacy, he dominated the French King Louis VII and overawed the Scottish king and Counts of Toulouse and Flanders. Whilst Henry II perceived the importance of the trappings of power as well as well as displays of pageantry and splendour, as demonstrated by his show case castle at Dover; Henry II was more interested in wielding actual over the perception of power. As Prof David Carpenter states (2015, p190) Henry's overriding aim was to rebuild royal power after its' disintegration under his predecessor.

Henry II remained a vigorous and active ruler up until his final few weeks of life. Even very close to the end he managed to exert himself to action and in this activity we must pay him tribute. A less dedicated and strong will person might not have been able to work this hard so close to their death. In part, this activity was one of his greatest successes. People would remain loyal to Henry II, not because they loved or admired him, but because he would be guaranteed to move swiftly and decisively. His rapid movements around his vast domain was also instrumental in this regard; he could and would appear unexpectedly anywhere at any time.

He did however appear to have less success in addressing the needs and demands of his sons. Henry II gave his son Henry the Young King everything; except what he most desired – lands of his own to govern. Richard and Geoffrey on the other hand were given lands and title at early age, but seemed unable to recognise that they would then resent when Henry II decided to attempt to manoeuvre them like pawns on a chess board.

Henry II could be described as an 'absolute monarch'. He ruled through a personal form of kingship that relied most of all on his own authority and power. Henry II was reliant on no one individual, but as an absolute monarch, it could be considered to be somewhat strange then that Henry II helped to establish the basis for the English legal law we have today.

On the one hand Henry II could be described as a harsh king. He had little or no genuine concern for the peasantry and poor of his lands, and generally equated his own prosperity with that of the kingdom; if he was wealthy and powerful it meant that his lands and people were in good condition themselves. This would overlook some of the grievances his subjects had, particularly his tenants-in-chief. And yet, to some extent this was indeed the case. Henry II was most wealthy and powerful when his lands and people were experiencing stability and peace. Therefore Henry II worked hard to ensure that his lands, and in particular England was indeed stable and peaceful. This stability was often helped by legal reforms and Henry II was widely credited as the founding father of English Common Law. According to Professor David Carpenter (2015 p190) Henry;

"...in developing the legal actions of the common law, Henry did more than any king in the medieval period to create a solid base for monarchy – a base that reached out beyond the baronage to the knights and free tenants who were the main users and beneficiaries of the procedures".

The establishment of the circuit judges was an essential part of this. As king Henry II's justice was greatly in demand; but he could not be everywhere at once and by the establishment of itinerant judges, appointed by him on regional circuits ensured that his justice could reach more people more quickly. This meant that those who appealed to the king's justice could receive it and those who acted criminally were more likely to receive this justice too.

Another contribution to the future development of the nation of England that Henry II helped to create was to begin to establish permanent political institutions. Although the bulk of central government travelled across his lands in company with Henry II, the sheer scale of his large domains meant that local centres of power developed under his reign and with his approval. These institutions emerged across Normandy, Aquitaine, Anjou and Brittany, but particularly in England. Increasingly, the machinery of government was based at Westminster and London – where the government could run for years smoothly and well in his absence.

And yet, for all of these achievements Henry II died in a way that does not seem to fit the description of the ruler just provided above. He died, as the historian Antonia Fraser states, believing that he was a failure; betrayed by all of his sons and surrendering many concessions to the French King Philip Augustus.

TASK: A View of Henry II

The historian Antonia Fraser states that Henry II died believing he was a failure.

- *What do you think she meant by this statement?*
- *To what extent do you agree with her view?*

Spend no more than 30 minutes on this question

TASK: Another View of Henry II

The historian David Carpenter states that Henry II was a 'bully with brains and brawn'.

- *What do you think he meant by this statement?*
- *To what extent do you agree with his view?*

Spend no more than 30 minutes on this question

References, Glossary, timeline and ruler lists

Glossary

Afforestation - An act to make an area of land part of the royal forest and subject to royal forest law.

Aid - A payment demanded by a lord or king from his tenants for knight service or a tax imposed by the king on his kingdom.

Amercement - essentially a fine imposed by a king or court of law

Angevin Empire - The territory ruled by the Angevin kings.

Angevins - literally 'relating to Anjou'. A term used by historians to refer to the reigns of the kings Henry II (1154-1189), Richard I (1189-1199) and John (1199-1216).

Assize - legislation or a legal action.

Baron - A 'Great Man'. A title of minor nobility among Latin Europeans, a lord of a castle or manor.

Bailiwick – A local area such as a County, subject to the authority of an official such as a Sheriff.

Chancery - An office that accompanies the king, whose clerks sealed the king's charters, writs and letters.

Chief Justiciar - Chief Minister. In charge of the king's government in the absence of the king.

County - principal division of a kingdom. In England there were 38 Counties by 1215.

Count - A title of nobility among Latin Europeans, denoting a ruler of a region or province. In England the term Earl is used for Count.

Darrein presentment - a legal action was related to the privilege of a landowner, often associated with a fee, of the right to appoint a caretaker or parson to a particular parish.

Duke - A title of high nobility among Latin Europeans, denoting a ruler of a region or province often granted to a relation to the ruler of the Kingdom or Empire.

Earl - English Count.

Exchequer - Usually based at Westminster, a central institution of government that calculates and audits the king's yearly revenues.

Eyre: A visit by the King's justices in a locality to deal with any judicial proceedings.

Farm - A tax payment owed for by a piece of land, town, forest or county.

Glanvill - The book of laws and customs of England compiled between 1187-1189 produced under the supervision of Henry II's chief justiciar Ranulf de Glanvill.

Hundred – an administrative subdivision of the country. Approximately 650 Hundreds in England. Also called Wapentakes in some areas such as Lincolnshire and Yorkshire.

Itinerant Judges: Judges that tour the counties in the six judicial circuits.

Justiciar - Chief Minister. In charge of the king's government in an area in the absence of the king.

Knight - A mounted warrior and title of minor nobility.

Knight Service – A form of service whereby a tenant provides the service of a knight (or a number of knights) in return for the land they hold in possession.

Magnate - A general term for a great lord.

Mort d'ancestor – A common law legal action by which a free individual could access the inheritances bequeathed to them by relations who had died.

Novel disseisin or 'recent dispossession' was an action to recover lands of which the complainant had been dispossessed *(disseised)*.

Outremer - The 'lands beyond the seas' the lands conquered by the Latin Christians during the Crusades.

Patriarch - The highest ranking Christian Church Bishops.

Penny - A silver coin and the only coin in circulation. 12 pennies = 1 schilling, 160 pennies = 1 Mark and 240 pennies = 1 pound.

Pilgrim - An individual undertaking a journey of religious significance to a Holy site.

Pope - The Bishop of Rome. The leading Churchman of Europe.

Pound - A financial unit. 240 pennies = 1 pound, 20 schillings = 1 pound. 1 mark = 2/3 of 1 pound.

Relief - A payment made by a tenant to a lord in order to gain possession of an inheritance.

Seisin – A possession; typically of land. To be put into seisin is to give possession.

Serjeant - A professional infantry or cavalry soldier of non-noble rank in a Latin Christian army.

Sheriff - The king's local official in charge of an administrative area such as a County. They were appointed by the king and were responsible for security, tax collection and overseeing local courts.

Tenant – An individual that is in possession of land or property theoretically owned by another.

Tenement – a land holding.

Timeline of Henry II and his reign

Year	Event
1133 – 5th March	Henry born at Le Mans, son of Geoffrey Plantagenet and Matilda, former Empress of Germany.
1135 – 1st December	King HENRY I of England dies in Normandy
1135 – 22nd December	STEPHEN is acclaimed King of the English at Winchester
1136	Geoffrey Plantagenet invades Normandy
1138	Civil war in England begins
1140	Matilda comes to England to contest STEPHEN's kingship.
1141	STEPHEN captured at Lincoln, Matilda ousted from London.
1142	Henry comes to England aged 9 accompanied by 300 knights. Henry educated at Bristol.
1144	Geoffrey Plantagenet completes conquest of Normandy
1147	Henry attempts to invade England, aged 14
1148	Matilda leaves England
1149	Henry goes to Scotland and is knighted by King DAVID of Scotland at Carlisle, Henry fails to capture York
1150 – January	Henry becomes Duke of Normandy
1151 – August	Henry pays homage to King LOUIS VII of France for Normandy
1151 – September	Geoffrey Plantagenet dies aged 39. Henry becomes Count of Anjou
1152 – 18th May	Henry marries Eleanor of Aquitaine and becomes Duke of Aquitaine and Count of Poitiers as a result of this marriage

1153	1st son William born to HENRY II and Eleanor of Aquitaine
1153 – January	Henry invades England
1153 – December	Treaty of Westminster between Henry and STEPHEN. Henry to become King of England after the death of STEPHEN
1154 – October	STEPHEN dies
1154 – 19th December	HENRY crowned KING HENRY II of England at Westminster aged 21.
1155 – September	2nd son Henry (the Young King) born to HENRY II and Eleanor of Aquitaine
1156	HENRY II's brother Geoffrey rebels in Anjou
	Death of William eldest son of HENRY II and Eleanor of Aquitaine
1156 – June	1st daughter Matilda born
1157	HENRY II's brother Geoffrey ends rebellion and is invited to become Duke of Brittany
1158	HENRY II's brother Geoffrey dies and HENRY II Seizes control of the Duchy of Brittany
1158 – September	4th son Geoffrey born to HENRY II and Eleanor of Aquitaine
1159 June-September	HENRY II attacks city of Toulouse. Siege is unsuccessful.
1162	2nd daughter Eleanor born
1162	Thomas Becket becomes Archbishop of Canterbury
1163 – October	The Council of Westminster
1164 – January	The Council of Clarendon
1165	3rd daughter Joan born
1166	*Cartae Baronum*
1167	5th son John born to HENRY II and Eleanor of Aquitaine

1170	Henry the Young King crowned at York
1170 – 29th December	Thomas Becket murdered
1171	HENRY II in Ireland
1173	THE GREAT REBELLION
1183	Henry the Young King dies
1184	Richard forced to relinquish some control of Aquitaine
1186	Geoffrey dies
1187	Jerusalem is captured by Saladin. Third Crusade called. Richard takes the Cross
1188	HENRY II at war with KING PHILIP of France and Richard. Both HENRY II and KING PHILIP of France take the Cross
1189 – 4th July	Peace agreement between HENRY II, PHILIP of France and Richard.
1189 – 6th July	HENRY II dies at Chinon

Appendix 1: Documentary sources

Document 1: The Constitutions of Clarendon issued 1164

"In the year 1164 from the Incarnation of our Lord, in the fourth year of the papacy of Alexander, in the tenth year of the most illustrious king of the English, Henry II, in the presence of that same king, this memorandum or inquest was made of some part of the customs and liberties and dignities of his predecessors, viz., of king Henry his grandfather and others, which ought to be observed and kept in the kingdom. And on account of the dissensions and discords which had arisen between the clergy and the Justices of the lord king, and the barons of the kingdom concerning the customs and dignities, this inquest was made in the presence of the archbishops and bishops, and clergy and counts, and barons and chiefs of the kingdom. And these customs, recognized by the archbishops and bishops and counts and barons and by the nobler ones and elders of the kingdom... (A long list of Archbishops, Bishops, Earls and Counts omitted) and many other chiefs and nobles of the kingdom, clergy as well as laity.

A certain part, moreover, of the customs and dignities of the kingdom which were examined into, is contained in the present writing. Of which part these are the paragraphs;

1. If a controversy concerning advowson and presentation of churches arise between laymen, or between laymen and clerks, or between clerks, it shall be treated of and terminated in the court of the lord king.

2. Churches of the fee of the lord king cannot, unto all time, be given without his assent and concession.

3. Clerks charged and accused of anything, being summoned by the Justice of the king, shall come into his court, about to respond there for what it seems to the king's court that he should respond there; and in the ecclesiastical court for what it seems he should respond there; so that the Justice of the king shall send to the court of the holy church to see in what manner the affair will there be carried on. And if the clerk shall be convicted, or shall confess, the church ought not to protect him further.

4. It is not lawful for archbishops, bishops, and persons of the kingdom to go out of the kingdom without the permission of the lord king. And if it please the king and they go out, they shall give assurance that neither in going, nor in making a stay, nor in returning, will they seek the hurt or harm of king or kingdom.

5. The excommunicated shall not give a pledge as a permanency, nor take an oath, but only a pledge and surety of presenting themselves before the tribunal of the church, that they may be absolved.

6. Laymen ought not to be accused unless through reliable and legal accusers and witnesses in the presence of the bishop, in such wise that the archdean do not lose his right, nor any thing which he ought to have from it. And if those who are inculpated are such that no one wishes or dares to accuse them, the sheriff, being requested by the bishop, shall cause twelve lawful men of the neighbourhood or town to swear in the presence of the bishop that they will make manifest the truth in this matter, according to their conscience.

7. No one who holds of the king in chief, and no one of his demesne servitors, shall be excommunicated, nor shall the lands of any one of them be placed under an interdict, unless first the lord king, if he be in the land, or his Justice, if he be without the kingdom, be asked to do justice concerning him: and in such way that what shall pertain to the king's court shall there be terminated; and with regard to that which concerns the ecclesiastical court, he shall be sent thither in order that it may there be treated of.

8. Concerning appeals, if they shall arise, from the archdean they shall proceed to the bishop, from the bishop to the archbishop. And if the archbishop shall fail to render justice, they must come finally to the lord king, in order that by his command the controversy may be terminated in the court of the archbishop, so that it shall not proceed further without the consent of the lord king.

9. If a quarrel arise between a clerk and a layman or between a layman and a clerk concerning any tenement which the clerk wishes to attach to the church property but the layman to a lay fee: by the inquest of twelve lawful men, through the judgment of the chief Justice of the king, it shall be determined, in the presence of the Justice himself, whether the tenement belongs to the church property, or to the lay fee. And if it be recognized as belonging to the church property, the case shall be pleaded in the ecclesiastical court; but if to the lay fee, unless both are holders from the same bishop or baron, the case shall be pleaded in the king's court. But if both vouch to warranty for that fee before the same bishop or baron, the case shall be pleaded in his court; in such way that, on account of the inquest made, he who was first in possession shall not lose his seisin, until, through the pleading, the case shall have been proven.

10. Whoever shall belong to the city or castle or fortress or demesne manor of the lord king, if he be summoned by the archdean or bishop for any offense for which he ought to respond to them, and he be unwilling to answer their summonses, it is perfectly right to place him under the interdict; but he ought not to be excommunicated until the chief servitor of the lord king of that town shall be asked to compel him by law to answer the summonses. And if the servitor of the king be negligent in this matter, he himself shall be at the mercy of the lord king, and the bishop may thenceforth visit the man who was accused with ecclesiastical justice.

11. Archbishops, bishops, and all persons of the kingdom who hold of the king in chief have their possessions of the lord king as a barony, and answer for them to the Justices and servitors of the king, and follow and perform all the customs and duties as regards the king; and, like other barons, they ought to be present with the barons at the judgments of the court of the lord king, until it comes to a judgment to loss of life or limb.

12. When an archbishopric is vacant, or a bishopric, or an abbey, or a priory of the demesne of the king, it ought to be in his hand; and he ought to receive all the revenues and incomes from it, as demesne ones. And, when it comes to providing for the church, the lord king should summon the more important persons of the church, and, in the lord king's own chapel, the election ought to take place with the assent of the lord king and with the counsel of the persons of the kingdom whom he had called for this purpose. And there, before he is consecrated, the person elected shall do homage and fealty to the lord king as to his liege lord, for his life and his members and his earthly honours, saving his order.

13. If any of the nobles of the kingdom shall have dispossessed an archbishop or bishop or archdean, the lord king should compel them personally or through their families to do justice. And if by chance any one shall have dispossessed the lord king of his right, the archbishops and bishops and archdeans ought to compel him to render satisfaction to the lord king.

14. A church or cemetery shall not, contrary to the king's justice, detain the chattels of those who are under penalty of forfeiture to the king, for they (the chattels) are the king's, whether they are found within the churches or without them.

15. Pleas concerning debts which are due through the giving of a bond, or without the giving of a bond, shall be in the jurisdiction of the king.

16. The sons of rustics may not be ordained without the consent of the lord on whose land they are known to have been born.

Moreover, a record of the aforesaid royal customs Anna dignities has been made by the foresaid Archbishops and Bishops, and Counts and Barons, and nobles and elders of the kingdom, at Clarendon on the fourth day before the Purification of the blessed Mary the perpetual Virgin; the lord Henry being there present with his father the lord king. There are, moreover, many other and great customs and dignities of the holy mother church, and of the lord king, and of the barons of the kingdom, which are not contained in this writ. And may they be preserved to the holy church, and to the lord king, and to his heirs, and to the barons of the kingdom, and may they be inviolably observed for ever."

Document 2: The Assize of Clarendon 1166

Assize of Clarendon 1166

Here begins the Assize of Clarendon made by King Henry II., with the assent of archbishops, bishops, abbots, earls, and barons of all England.

1. In the first place the said King Henry ordained on the advice of all his barons, for preserving peace and maintaining justice, that inquiry be made through the several counties and through the several hundreds by twelve more lawful men of the hundred and by four more lawful men of each vill, upon oath that they will tell the truth, whether in their hundred or in their vill there is any man cited or charged as himself being a robber or murderer or thief or anyone who has been a receiver of robbers or murderers or thieves since the lord king was king. And let the justices inquire this before themselves and the sheriffs before themselves.

2. And he who shall be found by the oath of the aforesaid cited or charged as having been a robber or murderer or thief or a receiver of them since the lord king was king, let him be arrested and go to the judgment of water, and let him swear that he was not a robber or murderer or thief or a receiver of them since the lord king was king, to the value of five shillings so far as he knows.

3. And if the lord of him who was arrested or his steward or his men demand him by pledge within the third day after his arrest, let him be given up and his chattels until he make his law.

4. And when a robber or murderer or thief or the receivers of them be arrested through the aforesaid oath, if the justices are not to come quite soon into the county where the arrests have been made, let the sheriffs send word by some intelligent man to one of the nearer justices that such men have been taken; and the justices shall send back word to the sheriffs where they wish to have the men brought before them; and the sheriffs shall bring them before the justices; and also they shall bring with them from the hundred and the vill where the arrests have been made two lawful men to carry the record of the county and hundred as to why the men were arrested, and there before the justices let them make their law.

5. And in the case of those who are arrested by the aforesaid oath of this assize no one is to have court or justice or chattels except the lord king in his court before his justices, and the lord king shall have all their chattels. But as to those who have been arrested otherwise than by this oath, let it be as it is accustomed and ought to be.

6. And let the sheriffs who have arrested them bring them before the justice without any other summons than they shall have from him. And when robbers, murderers, thieves, or their receivers, who have been arrested through the oath or otherwise, are turned over to the sheriffs, they are forthwith to receive them without delay.

7. And in the several counties where there are no jails, let them be made in a borough or in some castle of the king at the king's expense and from his wood if it is near, or from some neighbouring wood, on the estimation of the king's servants, to the end that the sheriffs may keep in them those who have been arrested by the officers whose function it is to do this and by their servants.

8. Also it is the king's will that all come to the county courts to make this oath, so that no one stay away on account of any immunity which he has or court or jurisdiction which he has held; but they are to come to make this oath.

9. And let there not be any one within a castle or outside a castle, or indeed in the honour of Wallingford, who shall refuse to let the sheriffs enter his court or his land to view the frank-pledges and to see that all are under pledges; and let them be sent before the sheriffs under a free pledge.

10. And let no one in the cities or boroughs have men or receive them into his house, land, or jurisdiction, whom he will not undertake to produce before the justice if they are sought; or else let him be in frank-pledge.

11. And let there be no one in city or borough, inside or outside a castle, or in the honour of Wallingford who shall deny entrance to the sheriffs into their land or jurisdiction for the purpose of arresting those who have been cited or charged as being robbers or murderers or thieves or the receivers of them, or outlaws or those cited in a matter touching the forest; but it is commanded that they help them in making the arrest.

12. And if anyone be taken who has the spoil of his robbery or theft in his possession, if he bear an ill name and have a notoriously bad reputation, and have no warrant, let him not have law. But if he be not suspected on account of what he has in his possession, let him go to the water.

13. And if any one, in the presence of lawful men or the hundreds, make confession of robbery, murder, theft, or the reception of those committing them, and should later wish to deny it, let him not have law.

14. Moreover the lord king wills that those who make their law and are quit thereby, if they have a very bad reputation and are publicly and scandalously decried on the testimony of many lawful men, shall forswear the king's lands, to the effect that within eight days they shall cross the sea unless the wind detain them; and with the first wind which they have thereafter they shall cross the sea, and they shall never return to England unless by the grace of the lord king; and there let them be outlaws, and if they return let them be taken as outlaws.

15. And the lord king forbids that any waif, that is to say a vagrant or unknown person, be given lodging with anyone except in a borough; and he is not to be lodged there except for one night, unless he be sick while there or his horse, so that he is able to show an evident excuse.

16. And if he should stay there more than one night, he is to be arrested and held until his lord come to stand pledge for him, or until he himself secure good pledges; and he who lodged him is also to be arrested.

17. And if a sheriff send word to another sheriff that men have fled from his county to the other county because of robbery, murder, theft, or the reception of those committing them, or for outlawry or an offense against the king's forest, let the latter sheriff arrest them; and indeed if he find out of himself or through others that such men have fled into his county, he is to arrest and hold them until he have sure pledges for them.

18. And let all the sheriffs make a list of all fugitives who have fled from their counties; and let them do this before the county courts, and they shall bring the names of these men in writing before the justices when first they come to them, in order that they may be sought throughout all England and their chattels seized for the benefit of the king.

19. And the lord king wills that as soon as the sheriffs receive the summonses of the itinerant justices to be before them with their county courts, they shall assemble their county courts and find out all who have recently come into their counties, since this assize; and they are to send these away under pledges to appear before the justices, or else keep them in custody until the justices come to them, and then produce them before the justices.

20. Also the lord king forbids monks or canons or any monastic house to receive any of the lower class of people as monk, canon, or brother until his reputation be known, unless he be sick unto death.

21. Moreover the lord king forbids that any one in all England should receive into his land or jurisdiction or any house of his, any of the sect of those apostates who have been excommunicated and branded at Oxford. And if any one receives them he shall be in the mercy of the lord king; and the house in which they were shall be carried outside the vill and burned. And every sheriff shall take oath to maintain this, and he shall cause to take the same oath all his ministers and the baron's stewards, and all the knights and freeholders of the counties.

22. And the lord king wills that this assize be held in his kingdom as long as it shall please him.

Document 3: Roger of Hovedon's account of the Great Rebellion (selected excerpts)

Roger of Hoveden was a clerk in the service of Henry II who wrote a History of England in the early years of the thirteenth century. As a royal clerk he was well-placed to gather information from members of the royal court.

"In the year of grace 1173, being the nineteenth year of the reign of king Henry, son of the empress Matilda, the said king was, on the day of the Nativity of our Lord, at Chinon, in Anjou, and queen Eleanor was there with him, while the king, his son, and his wife were in Normandy...

...the king of England, the father, and the king, the son, came together to Limoges; and thither Raymond, Count of Toulouse, came, and there did homage to both the kings of England, and to Richard, Earl of Poitiers, for Toulouse, to hold the same of them by hereditary right...

...the king of England intended to grant to his son John; and on the king expressing an intention to give him the castle of Chinon, the castle of Loudon, and the castle of Mirabeau, the king, his son, would in nowise agree thereto, nor allow it to be done. For he was already greatly offended that his father was unwilling to assign to him some portion of his territories, where he, with his wife, might take up their residence. Indeed, he had requested his father to give him either Normandy, or Anjou, or England, which request he had made at the suggestion of the king of France, and of those of the earls and barons of England and Normandy who disliked his father: and from this time it was that the king, the son, had been seeking pretexts and an opportunity for withdrawing from his father. And he had now so entirely revolted in feeling from obeying his wishes, that he could not even converse with him on any subject in a peaceable manner.

Having now gained his opportunity, both as to place and occasion, the king, the son, left his father, and proceeded to the king of France. However, Richard Barre, his chancellor, Walter, his chaplain, Ailward, his chamberlain, and William Blund, his apparitor, left him, and returned to the king, his father. Thus did the king's son lose both his feelings and his senses; he repulsed the innocent, persecuted a father, usurped authority, seized upon a kingdom, he alone was the guilty one, and yet a whole army conspired against his father; "so does the madness of one make many mad." For he it was who thirsted for the blood of a father, the gore of a parent!

In the meantime, Louis, king of France, held a great council at Paris, at which he and all the principal men of France made oath to the son of the king of England that they would assist him in every way in expelling his father from the kingdom, if he should not accede to his wishes: on which he swore to them that he would not make peace with his father, except with their sanction and consent. After this, he swore that he would give to Philip, Count of Flanders, for his homage, a £1000 of yearly revenues in England, and the whole of Kent, together with Dover castle, and Rochester castle; to Matthew, Count of Boulogne, for his homage, Kirkeketon in Lindsey, and the Earldom of Mortaigne..; and to Theobald, Count of Blois, for his homage, £200 of yearly revenues in Anjou, and the castle of Amboise, with all the jurisdiction which he had claimed to hold in Touraine and he also quitted claim to him of all right that the king his father and himself had claimed in Chateau Regnaud. All these gifts, and many besides that he made to other persons, he confirmed under his new seal, which the king of France had ordered to be made for him.

Besides these, he made other gifts, which, under the same seal, he confirmed, namely, to William, king of

Scotland, for his assistance, the whole of Northumberland as far as the river Tyne. To the brother of the same king he gave for his services the Earldom of Huntingdon and of Cambridgeshire and to Earl Hugh Bigot, for his services, the castle of Norwich.

Immediately after Easter, in 1173, the whole of the kingdom of France, and the king, the son of the king of England, Richard his brother, Count of Poitiers, and Geoffrey, Earl of Brittany, and nearly all the Earls and barons of England, Normandy, Aquitaine, Anjou, and Brittany, arose against the king of England the father, and laid waste his lands on every side with fire, sword, and rapine: they also laid siege to his castles, and took them by storm, and there was no one to relieve them. Still, he made all the resistance against them that he possibly could: for he had with him 20,000 Brabanters (mercenaries) who served him faithfully, but not without large pay which he gave them...

...Accordingly, immediately after Easter, as previously mentioned, the wicked fury of the traitors burst forth. For, raving with diabolical frenzy, they laid waste the territories of the king of England on both sides of the sea with fire and sword in every direction. Philip, Count of Flanders, with a large army, entered Normandy, and laid siege to Aumarle, and took it. Proceeding thence, he laid siege to the castle of Drincourt, which was surrendered to him ...

In the meantime, Louis, King of France, and the king of England, the son, laid siege to Verneuil; but Hugh de Lacy and Hugh de Beauchamp, who were the constables thereof, defended the town of Verneuil boldly and with resolute spirit. In consequence of this, the king of France, after remaining there a whole month, with difficulty took a small portion of the town on the side where his engines of war had been planted. There were in Verneuil, besides the castle, three burghs; each of which was separated from the other and enclosed with a strong all and a foss filled with water. One of these was called the Great Burgh, beyond the walls of which were pitched the tents of the king of France and his engines of war. At the end of this month, when the burghers in the Great Burgh saw that food and necessaries were failing them, and that they should have nothing to eat, being compelled by hunger and want, they made a truce for three days with the king of France, for the purpose of going to their lord the king of England, in order to obtain succour of him; and they made an agreement that if they should not have succour within the next three days, they would surrender to him that burgh.

They then gave hostages to the king of France to the above effect, and the king of France, the king of England, the son, and Count Robert, the brother of the king of France, Count Henry de Trois, Theobald, Count of Blois, and William, archbishop of Sens, made oath to them, that if they should surrender the burgh to the king of France at the period named, the king of France would restore to them their hostages free and unmolested, and would do no injury to them, nor allow it to be done by others. This composition having been made to the above effect, the burgesses before mentioned came to their lord the king of England, and announced to him the agreement which they had made with the king of France and the king his son.

On hearing of this, the king of England collected as large an army as he possibly could from Normandy and the rest of his dominions, and came to Breteuil, a castle belonging to Robert, Earl of Leicester, which the Earl himself, taking to flight on his approach, left without any protection. This the king entirely reduced to ashes, and the next day, for the purpose of engaging with the king of France, proceeded to a high hill, near Verneuil, with the whole of his army, and drew up his troops in order of battle. This too was the peremptory day upon which that portion of Verneuil was to be surrendered if it did not obtain succour.

Upon this, Louis, king of the Franks, sent...to the king of England, the father, who appointed an interview to be held between them on the morrow; and the king of England, to his misfortune, placed confidence in them; for he was deceived. For on the morrow the king of France neither came to the interview, nor yet sent any messenger. On this, the king of England sent out spies to observe the position of the king of France and his army; but while the spies were delaying their return that portion of Verneuil was surrendered to the king of France to which he had laid siege. However, he did not dare retain it in his hands, having transgressed the oath which he had made to the burghers. For he neither restored to them their hostages, nor preserved the peace as he had promised; but, entering the town, made the burghers prisoners, carried off their property, set fire to the Burgh, and then, taking to flight, carried away with him the burghers before-mentioned into France.

When word was brought of this to the king of England, he pursued them with the edge of the sword, slew many of them, and took considerable numbers, and at nightfall arrived at Verneuil, where he remained one night, and ordered the walls which had been levelled to be rebuilt. But, in order that these events may be kept in memory, it is as well to know that this flight of the king of France took place on the fifth day before the ides of August, being the fifth day of the week, upon the vigil of Saint Laurence, to the praise and glory of our Lord Jesus Christ, who by punishing the crime of perfidy, so speedily avenged the indignity done to his Martyr.

On the following day, the king of England, the father, left Verneuil, and took the castle of Damville, which belonged to Gilbert de Tilieres, and captured with it a great number of knights and men-at-arms. After this, the king came to Rouen, and thence dispatched his Brabanters, in whom he placed more confidence than the rest, into Brittany, against Hugh, Earl of Chester, and Ralph de Fougeres, who had now gained possession of nearly the whole of it. When these troops approached, the Earl of Chester and Ralph de Fougeres went forth to meet them. In consequence of this, preparations were made for battle; the troops were drawn out in battle array, and everything put in readiness for the combat. Accordingly, the engagement having commenced, the enemies of the king of England were routed, and the men of Brittany were laid pros. bate and utterly defeated. The Earl, however, and Ralph de Fougeres, with many of the most powerful men of Brittany, shut themselves up in the fort of Dol, which they had taken by stratagem; on which, the Brabanters besieged them on every side, on the thirteenth day before the calends of September, being the second day of the week. In this battle there were taken by the Brabanters seventeen knights remarkable for their valour ... . Besides these, many others were captured; both horse and foot, and more than fifteen hundred of the Bretons were slain.

Now, on the day after this capture and slaughter, "Rumour, than which nothing in speed more swift exists," reached the ears of the king of England, who, immediately setting out on his march towards Dol, arrived there on the fifth day of the week, and immediately ordered his stone-engines, and other engines of war, to be got in readiness. The Earl of Chester, however, and those who were with him in the fort, being unable to defend it, surrendered it to the king, on the seventeenth day before the calends of September, being the Lord's Day ; and, in like manner, the whole of Brittany, with all its fortresses, was restored to him, and its chief men were carried into captivity. In the fortress of Dol many knights and yeomen were taken prisoners ... After these victories which God granted to the king of England, the son of the empress Matilda, the king of France and his supporters fell into despondency, and used all possible endeavours, that peace might be made between the king of England and his sons. In consequence of this, there was at length a meeting between Gisors and Trie, at which Louis, king of the Franks, attended, accompanied by the archbishops, bishops, earls; and barons of his realm, and bringing with him Henry, Richard, and Geoffrey, the sons of the king of England. Henry, king of England, the father, attended, with the archbishops, bishops, earls, and barons of his dominions.

A conference was accordingly held between him and his sons, for the purpose of establishing peace, on the seventh day before the calends of October, being the third day of the week. At this conference, the king, the father, offered to the king, his son, a moiety of the revenues of his demesnes in England, and four fitting castles in the same territory; or, if his son should prefer to remain in Normandy, the king, the father, offered a moiety of the revenues of Normandy, and all the revenues of the lands that were his father's, the earl of Anjou, and three convenient castles in Normandy, and one fitting castle in Anjou, one fitting castle in Maine, and one fitting castle in Touraine. To his son Richard, also, he offered a moiety of the revenues of Aquitaine, and four fitting castles in the same territory. And to his son Geoffrey he offered all the lands that belonged, by right of inheritance, to the daughter of duke Conan, if he should, with the sanction of our lord the pope, be allowed to marry the above-named lady. The king, the father, also submitted himself entirely to the arbitration of the archbishop of Tarento and the legates of our lord the pope, as to adding to the above as much more of his revenues, and giving the same to his sons, as they should pronounce to be reasonable, reserving to himself the administration of justice and the royal authority.

But it did not suit the purpose of the king of France that the king's sons should at present make peace with their father: in addition to which, at the same conference, Robert, Earl of Leicester, uttered much opprobrious and abusive language to the king of England, the father, and laid his hand on his sword for the purpose of striking the king; but he was hindered by the bystanders from so doing, and the conference was immediately brought to a close.

On the day after the conference, the knights of the king of France had a skirmish with the knights of the king of England, between Curteles and Gisors; in which fight Ingelram, castellan of Trie, was made prisoner by Earl William de Mandeville, and presented to the king, the father. In the meantime, Robert, Earl of Leicester, having raised a large army, crossed over into England, and was received by Earl Hugh Bigot in the castle of Fremingham, where he supplied him with all necessaries. After this, the said Robert, Earl of Leicester, laid siege to Hakeneck, the castle of Ranulph de Broc, and took it; for, at this period, Richard de Lucy, justiciary of England, and Humphrey de Bohun, the king's constable, had marched with a large army into Lothian, the territory of the king of Scotland for the purpose of ravaging it.

When, however, they heard of the arrival of the Earl of Leicester in England, they were greatly alarmed, and laying all other matters aside, gave and received a truce from the king of Scotland, and, after hostages were delivered on both sides for the preservation of peace until the feast of Saint Hilary, hastened with all possible speed to Saint Edmund's. Thither also came to them Reginald, earl of Cornwall, the king's uncle, Robert, Earl of Gloucester, and William, Earl of Arundel, On the approach of the festival of All Saints, the above-named Earl of Leicester withdrew from Fremingham for the purpose of marching to Leicester, and came with his army to a place near St. Edmund's, which is known as Fornham, situate on a piece of marshy ground, not far from the church of Saint Genevieve. On his arrival being known, the earls, with a considerable force, and Humphrey de Bohun with three hundred knights, soldiers of the king, went forth armed for battle to meet the earl of Leicester, carrying before them the banner of Saint Edmund the king and Martyr as their standard. The ranks being drawn up in battle array, by virtue of the aid of God and of his most glorious Martyr Saint Edmund, they attacked the line in which the earl of Leicester had taken his position, and in a moment, in the twinkling of an eye, the Earl of Leicester was vanquished and taken prisoner, as also his wife and Hugh des Chateaux, a nobleman of the kingdom of France, and all their might was utterly crushed.

There fell in this battle more than ten thousand Flemings, while all the rest were taken prisoners, and being thrown into prison in irons, were there starved to death. As for the Earl of Leicester and his wife and Hugh des Chateaux, and the rest of the more wealthy men who were captured with them, they were sent into Normandy to the king the father; on which the king placed them in confinement at Falaise, and Hugh, Earl of Chester, with them.

In the year of grace 1174, being the twentieth year of the reign of king Henry, son of the empress Matilda, the said Henry spent the festival of the Nativity of our Lord at Caen in Normandy, and a truce was made between him and Louis, king of the Franks, from the feast of Saint Hilary until the end of Easter ...In the meantime, Roger de Mowbray fortified his castle at Kinardeferie, in Axholme; and Hugh, bishop of Durham, fortified the castle of Alverton. After Easter, breaking the truce, Henry, the son of the king of England, and Philip, Count of Flanders, having raised a large army, determined to come over to England.

In the meantime, William, king of the Scots, came into Northumberland with a large force, and there with his

Scotch and Galloway men committed execrable deeds. For his men ripped asunder pregnant women, and, dragging forth the embryos, tossed them upon the points of lances. Infants, children, youths, aged men, all of both sexes, from the highest to the lowest, they slew alike without mercy or ransom. The priests and clergy they murdered in the very churches upon the altars. Consequently, wherever the Scots and the Galloway men came, horror and carnage prevailed. Shortly after, the king of the Scots sent his brother David to Leicester, in order to assist the troops of the Earl of Leicester; but before he arrived there, Reginald, Earl of Cornwall, and Richard de Lacy, justiciary of England, had burned the city of Leicester to the ground, together with its churches add buildings, with the exception of the castle...In the meanwhile, William, king of the Scots, laid siege to Carlisle, of which Robert de Vals had the safe keeping; and leaving a portion of his army to continue the siege, with the remainder of it he passed through Northumberland, ravaging the lands of the king and his barons. He took the castle of Liddel, the castle of Burgh, the castle of Appleby, the castle of Mercwrede, and the castle of Irebothe, which was held by Odonel de Umfraville, after which he returned to the siege of Carlisle. Here he continued the siege, until Robert decals, in consequence of provisions failing him and the other persons there, made a treaty with him on the following terms, namely, that, at the feast of Saint Michael next ensuing, he would surrender to him the castle and town of Carlisle, unless, in the meantime, he should obtain succour from his master the king of England.

On this, the king of the Scots, departing thence, laid siege to the castle of Prudhoe, which belonged to Odonel de Umfraville, but was unable to take it. For Robert de Stuteville, sheriff of York, William de Vesci, Ranulphe de Glanville, Ralph de Tilly, constable of the household of the archbishop of York, Bernard de Baliol, and Odonel de Umfraville, having assembled a large force, hastened to its succour.

On learning their approach, the king of Scotland retreated thence, and laid siege to the castle of Alnwick, which belonged to William de Vesci, and then, dividing his army into three divisions, kept one with himself, and gave the command of the other two to earl Dunecan and the earl of Angus, and Richard de Morville, giving them orders to lay waste the neighbouring provinces in all directions, slaughter the people, and carry off the spoil...

In the meantime, the king of England, the son, and Philip, Count of Flanders, came with a large army to Gravelines, for the purpose of crossing over to England. On hearing of this, the king of England, the father, who had marched with his army into Poitou, and had taken many fortified places and castles, together with the city of Saintes, and two fortresses there, one of which was called Fort Maror, as also the cathedral church of Saintes, which the knights and men-at-arms had strengthened against him with arms and a supply of provisions, returned into Anjou, and took the town of Ancenis, which belonged to Guion de Ancenis, near Saint Florence. On taking it, he strengthened it with very strong fortifications, and retained it in his own hands, and then laid waste the adjoining parts of the province with fire and sword; he also rooted up the vines and fruit-bearing trees, after which he returned into Normandy, while the king, his son, and Philip, Count of Flanders, were still detained at Gravelines, as the wind was contrary, and they were unable to cross over. On this, the king of England, the father, came to Barfleur where a considerable number of ships had been assembled against his arrival...Immediately on this, he embarked, and, on the following day, landed at Southampton, in England, on the eight day before the ides of July, being the second day of the week, bringing with him his wife, queen Eleanor, and queen Margaret, daughter of Louis, king of the Franks, and wife of his son Henry, with Robert, Earl of Leicester, and Hugh, Earl of Chester, whom he immediately placed in confinement.

On the day after this, he set out on a pilgrimage to the tomb of Saint Thomas the Martyr, archbishop of Canterbury. On his approach, as soon as he was in sight of the church, in which the body of the blessed martyr lay buried, he dismounted from the horse on which he rode, took off his shoes, and barefoot, and clad in woollen garments, walked three miles to the tomb of the martyr, with such humility and compunction of heart, that it may be believed beyond a doubt to have been the work of Him who looketh down on the earth, and maketh it to tremble. To those who beheld them, his footsteps, along the road on which he walked, seemed to be covered with blood, and really were so, for his tender feet being cut by the hard stones, a great quantity of blood flowed from them on to the ground. When he had arrived at the tomb, it was a holy thing to see the affliction which he suffered, with sobs and tears, and the discipline to which he submitted from the hands of the bishops and a great number of priests and monks. Here, also, aided by the prayers of many holy men, he passed the night, before the sepulchre of the blessed Martyr, in prayer, fasting, and lamentations. As for the gifts and revenues which, for the remission of his sins, he bestowed on this church, they can never under any circumstance be obliterated from the remembrance thereof. In the morning of the following day, after hearing mass, he departed thence, on the third day before the ides of July, being Saturday, with the intention of proceeding to London. And, inasmuch as he was mindful of the Lord in his entire heart, the Lord granted unto him the victory over his enemies, and delivered them captive into his hands.

For, on the very same Saturday on which the king left Canterbury, William, king of the Scots, was taken prisoner at Alnwick by the above-named knights of Yorkshire, who had pursued him after his retreat from Prudhoe. Thus, even thus; "How rarely is it that vengeance with halting step forsakes the pursuit of the wicked!" Together with him, there were taken prisoners...and many others, who voluntarily allowed themselves to be made prisoners, lest they might appear to have sanctioned the capture of their lord.

On the same day, Hugh, Count de Bar sur Seine, nephew of Hugh, bishop of Durham, effected a landing at Hartlepool with forty knights and five hundred Flemings, for whom the before-named bishop had sent, but in consequence of the capture of the king of Scotland, the bishop immediately allowed the said Flemings to return home, having first given them allowance and pay for forty days. Count Hugh, however, together with the knights who had come with him, he made to stay, and gave the castle of Alverton into their safe keeping...In the meantime, Louis, king of France, hearing that the king of England, the father, had crossed over, and that the king of Scots was taken prisoner, with whose misfortunes he greatly condoled, recalled the king of England the son, and Philip, Earl of Flanders, who were still staying at Gravelines; and after they had returned to him, laid siege to Rouen on all sides, except that on which the river Seine flows.

The king, the father, on hearing of the capture of the king of the Scots, rejoiced with exceeding great joy, and after a thanksgiving to Almighty God and the blessed martyr Thomas, set out for Huntingdon, and laid siege to the castle, which was surrendered to him on the Lord's day following, being the twelfth day before the calends of August. The knights and men-at-arms who were in the castle threw themselves on the king's mercy, safety being granted to life and limb. Immediately upon this, the king departed thence with his army towards Fremingham, the castle of Earl Hugh Bigot, where the Earl himself was, with a large body of Flemings. The king, on drawing nigh to Fremingham, encamped at a place which is called Seleham, and remained there that night. On the following day, Earl Hugh Bigot came to him, and, making a treaty of peace with him, surrendered to him the castle of Fremingham, and the castle of Bungay, and with considerable difficulty obtained the king's permission that the Flemings who were with him might without molestation return home....On the following day, namely, on the seventh day before the calends of August, the king departed from Seleham, and proceeded to Northampton; on his arrival at which place William, king of the Scots, was brought to him, with his feet fastened beneath a horse's belly. There also came to him Hugh bishop of Durham, who delivered to him possession of the castle of Durham, the castle of Norham, and the new castle of Alverton, which he had fortified, and, after considerable difficulty, obtained permission that his nephew, the Count de Bar, and the knights who had come with him, might return to their own country. Roger de Mowbray also came thither to him, and surrendered to him the castle of Tresk, and the Earl of Ferrers delivered up to him the castles of Tutesbury, and of Duffield; Anketill Mallory also and William de Dive, constables of the Earl of Leicester, surrendered to him the castles of Leicester, of Mountsorrel, and of Groby.

Thus then, within the space of three weeks, was the whole of England restored to tranquillity, and all its fortified places delivered into the king's hands. These matters being arranged to his satisfaction, he speedily crossed over from England to Normandy, and landed at Barfleur on the sixth day before the ides of August, being the fifth day of the week, taking with him his Brabanters and a thousand Welshmen, together with William, king of the Scots, Robert, Earl of Leicester, and Hugh, Earl of Chester, whom he placed in confinement, first at Caen, and afterwards at Falaise ... After this, on the Lord's day next ensuing, the king, the father, arrived with his Brabanters and Welshmen at Rouen, which the king of France and the king of England, the son, were besieging on one side, while on the other there was free egress and ingress. On the following morning, the king sent his Welshmen beyond the river Seine; who, making way by main force, broke through the midst of the camp of the king of France, and arrived unhurt at the great forest, and on the same day slew more than a hundred of the men of the king of France.

Now, the king of France had been staying there hardly a month, when, lo! the king of England, the father, coming from England, opened the gates of the city, which the burgesses had blocked up, and sallying forth with his knights and men-at-arms, caused the fosses which had been made between the army of the king of France and the city, to be filled up with logs of timber, stones, and earth, and to be thus made level. As for the king of France, he and his men remained in their tents, and were not inclined to come forth. The rest of the people of the king of England took up their positions for the defence of the walls, but no one attacked them; however, a part of the army of the king of France made an attempt to destroy their own engines of war.

On the following day, early in the morning, the king of France sent the weaker portion of his army into his own territories; and, with the permission of the king of England, followed them on the same day to a place which is called Malaunay and lies between Rouen and the town called Tostes; having first given security by the hand of William, archbishop of Sens, and of Count Theobald, that on the following day he would return to confer with the king of England on making peace between him and his sons. The king of France, however, did not keep his engagement and his oath, and did not come on the following day to the conference, but departed into his own territories.

However, after the expiration of a few days, he again sent the above-named archbishop of Sens and Count Theobald to the king of England, appointing a day for the conference, to be held at Gisors, on the Nativity of Saint Mary. When they met there they could not come to an agreement, on account of Richard, Count of Poitiers, who was at this time in Poitiers, besieging the castles and subjects of his father. In consequence of this, they again held another conference between them, upon the festival of Saint Michael, between Tours and Amboise, on which occasion they agreed to a truce on these terms: that the said Richard, earl of Poitou, should be excluded from all benefit of the truce, and that the king of France and the king of England, the son, should give him no succour whatever. Upon these arrangements being made on either side, the king of England, the father, moved on his army into Poitiers; on which, Richard, Count of Poitiers, his son, not daring to await his approach, fled from place to place. When he afterwards came to understand that the king of France, and the king, his brother, had excluded him from the benefit of the truce, he was greatly indignant thereat; and, coming with tears, he fell on his face upon the ground at the feet of his father, and imploring pardon, was received into his father's bosom. These events took place at Poitiers, on the eleventh day before the calends of October, being the second day of the week; and thus, the king and his son Richard becoming reconciled they entered the city of Poitiers.

After this, they both set out together for a conference held between Tours and Amboise, on the day before the calends of October, being the second day of the week and the day after the feast of Saint Michael. Here the king, the son, and Richard and Geoffrey, his brothers, by the advice and consent of the king and barons of France, made the treaty of peace underwritten with the king their father...

Document 4: The Assize of Northampton 1177

The Assize of Northampton 1177

1. If, by the oath of twelve knights of the hundred — or, should knights not be present, by the oath of twelve lawful freemen — and by the oath of four men of every vill in the hundred, any one has been accused in the presence of the lord king's justices of murder or theft or robbery, or of receiving men who have committed such (crimes), or of falsification[2] or arson, he shall go to the ordeal of water; and if he fails [in the ordeal], he shall lose one foot. And to increase the severity of the law, it was added at Northampton that with the foot he should lose his right hand, and that he should abjure the realm and depart from it within forty days. And if he should be cleared by the [ordeal of] water, let him find sureties and remain in the kingdom, unless he has been accused of murder or other disgraceful felony by the community (commune) of the county and the lawful knights of his own countryside (patria). If he has been accused in the aforesaid manner of this [sort of crime], although he has been cleared by the (ordeal of) water, let him nevertheless go out of the kingdom within forty days and take with him his chattels, saving the rights of his lords; and let him abjure the realm in the lord king's mercy. This assize, moreover, shall hold good for all the time since the assize was made at Clarendon down to the present, and henceforward during the lord king's pleasure, with regard to murder, treason, and arson, and with regard to all [offenses in] the preceding chapters, except minor thefts and robberies which were committed in time of war, as of horses, oxen, and lesser things.

2. No one, either in a vill or in a borough, shall be permitted to give lodging within his house for more than one night to any stranger for whom he is unwilling to be legally responsible, unless such lodger has a reasonable excuse which the master of the house may prove to his neighbours. And when he leaves, let him leave by day and in the presence of the neighbours.

3. If anyone has possessed (proceeds) of murder or theft or robbery or falsification, or of any other felony that he has committed, and confesses it before the reeve of a hundred or a borough and before lawful men, he may not afterwards deny it before the justices. And if, without possession, he admits anything of the same sort in their presence, this likewise he may not deny before the justices.

4. If any freeholder dies, his heirs shall remain in such seisin as their father had of his fee on the day that he was alive and dead; and they shall have his chattels, with which to carry out the testament of the deceased. And afterwards they shall go to their lord and shall perform to him their obligation for relief and other things owed from their fee. And if the heir is under age, the lord of the fee shall receive his homage and have wardship over him so long as is right. The other lords, if there are several, shall [also] receive his homage and he shall perform to them whatever obligations he owes. And the wife of the deceased shall have her dowry and the portion of his chattels to which she is entitled. And if the lord of the fee denies to the heirs of the deceased the seisin of the said deceased ['s property] which they demand, the justices of the lord king shall have recognition made in the matter by twelve lawful men, as to what seisin in this respect the deceased had on the day that he was alive and dead (mort d'ancestor) And according to the recognition thus made, those [justices] shall make restitution to his heirs. And if any one acts contrary to this (command), and is convicted of so doing, let him remain in the king's mercy.

5. The justices of the lord king shall have recognition made of disseisins contrary to the assize from the time that the lord king first came to England after the peace made between him and the king his son.

6. From the first Sunday after Easter to the first Sunday after Pentecost, the justices shall receive oaths of fealty to the lord king from all who wish to dwell in the kingdom: namely, from earls, barons, knights, freeholders, and even peasants. And whoever refuses to swear fealty is to be seized as an enemy of the lord king. The justices are also to command that all those who have not yet performed their homage and allegiance to the lord king shall come at the time assigned them and perform homage and allegiance to the king as to their liege lord.

7. The justices, by writ of the lord king or of those acting in his place, shall enforce all rights and claims pertaining to the lord king and his crown to the amount of half a knight's fee and less, unless the case is so important that it cannot be decided without the lord king or [unless it is] such as, through their own uncertainty, the justices may report to him or to those acting in his place. They should, however, to the best of their ability strive to assure the king's interest. Also they shall hold assize concerning wicked thieves and [other] malefactors of the land — which assize, by the counsel of the king his son and of his men, is [to be held] throughout the counties to which they shall go.

8. The justices shall see to it that the castles (that were supposed to have been) razed are totally razed, and that those to be razed are well pulled down. And if they fail to do this, the lord king wishes them brought to judgment in his court as men in contempt of his command.

9. The justices shall make inquiry concerning the escheats, churches, lands, and women who are in the gift of the lord king.

10.The bailiffs of the lord king shall be answerable at the exchequer both for their fixed rents and for all sums acquired within their bailiwicks, except those belonging to the (farm of the) county.

11.The justices shall make inquiry concerning the custody of castles: as to who owe, how much, and where. And afterwards they shall give the information to the lord king.

12. A thief, from the time that he is captured, shall be delivered to the sheriff to guard. And if the sheriff is absent, he shall be taken to the nearest castellan, and the latter shall guard him until he is turned over to the sheriff.

13. The justices shall have investigation made, according to the custom of the land, as to those who have left the kingdom; and unless they are willing to return within a stated time and to stand trial in the court of the lord king, they shall then be outlawed; and the names of the outlaws shall be brought to the exchequer at Easter and Michaelmas, and shall thence be sent to the lord king.

Notes on the Assize of Northampton

The Assize of Northampton was not a full replacement of the Assizes of Calrendon, rather a series of amendments and adjustments.

Falsoneria, meaning either counterfeiting or forgery.

The so-called illegal or adulterine castles are referred to in this assize.

The official in charge of a castle, was often called a constable.

Appendix 2: Select list of Rulers

Rulers of France

Philip I – 1060-1108

Louis VI – 1108-1137

Louis VII – 1137-1180

Philip II – 1180-1223

Rulers of England

William II – 1087-1100

Henry I – 1100-1135

Stephen – 1135-1154

Henry II – 1154-1189

Richard I – 1189-1199

John – 1199-1216

Rulers of Germany

Henry IV – 1056-1106

Henry V – 1106-1125

Lothar III – 1125-1137

Conrad III – 1138-1152

Frederick I – 1152-1190

Henry VI – 1190-1197

Philip of Swabia 1198-1208

Byzantine Emperors

Alexius I - 1081-1118

John II - 1118-1143

Manuel I – 1143-1180

Alexius II – 1180-1183

Andronicus – 1183-1185

Isaac II – 1185-1195 & 1203-4

Rulers of Jerusalem

Baldwin I - 1100-1118

Baldwin II - 1118-1131

Fulk - 1131-1143

Baldwin III - 1143-1163

Amalric – 1163-1174

Baldwin IV – 1174-1185

Baldwin V – 1185-1186

Guy of Lusignan – 1186-1192

Online Resources

www.bbc.co.uk/history/historic_figures/eleanor_of_aquitaine.shtml

www.history.com/topics/british-history/eleanor -of-aquitaine

www.oxfordreference.com

www.britannica.com

www.constitution.org

www.early englishlaws.ac.uk

www.fordham.edu/Halsall/sbook.asp

Bibliography

Asbridge, T. *The Greatest Knight* (Simon Schuster UK Ltd 2015)

Barlow, F. *The Feudal Kingdom of England 1042–1216* (Routledge, 1999).

Carpenter, D. *Magna Carta* (Penguin Classics 2015)

Castor, H. *She Wolves: The Women who ruled England Before Elizabeth* (Faber & Faber, 2010)

Fraser, A. *The Lives of the Kings and Queens of England* (Book Club Associates 1975)

Gillingham, J. *Richard I* (George Weidenfeld & Nielson Ltd 1973)

Gillingham, J. *The Angevin Empire*, (Bloomsbury Academic, 2000)

Guy, J. *Thomas Becket: Warrior, Priest, Rebel, Victim: A 900-Year-Old Story Retold* (Penguin 2013)

Henderson, E.F. *Select Historical Documents of the Middle Ages.* (London: George Bell and Sons, 1896)

Jones, D. *The Plantagenets* (William Collins 2012)

Poole, A.L. *From Domesday Book to Magna Carta, 1087–1216* (Oxford University Press, 1993)

Purser, T. *Medieval England 1042–1228* (Heinemann, 2004)

Stubbs, W. & Davis, H. W. C. eds., *Select Charters of English Constitutional History.* (Oxford: Clarendon Press, 1913)

About Athena Education Online

Athena Education Online is a specialist team of professional course writers based in Lincolnshire, UK. All course writers are specialists in their area and are all are experienced teachers and lecturers as well as experienced examination assessors for the main examination boards, including AQA, OCR, Edexcel and CIE.

About the Author

P Kenney is an experienced, course writer, college lecturer and tutor and examiner for several examination boards. A graduate of the University of Wales and postgraduate of Nottingham University in Classics, History and Archaeology, he has written critical guides for a range of historical and literary texts.

About the Editor

T Kenney is a teacher, examiner and moderator in English Literature and English Language and Literature. She is a postgraduate of Cambridge University and the Open University with a MA in Literature. She has written critical guides for a range of poetry, prose and drama texts.

Terms and Conditions of Use

Thank you for purchasing this product.

By purchasing this product you acknowledge that we the producers of these materials are not affiliated with any educational institution, that this product is authorised by, sponsored by, or affiliated with any educational institution.

Use of this product does not ensure any expected exam grade of anyone owning or using this product. Neither do Athena Online Education guarantee that this product is affiliated with, or suitable for, any particular examination board or examination unit, however Athena Online Education will strive to ensure that all of its products match as closely as possible the qualification for which it is intended to support.

that Athena Online Education endorses these websites and resources in any way.

Printed in Great Britain
by Amazon

49778828R00129